Praise for
BRILLIANT OR BLUNDER

"Challenge is the opportunity for greatness, and in *Brilliant or Blunder* by Mary Lippitt, you will discover the mindsets that leaders must have to navigate current challenges and turn them into exciting opportunities. This is fresh, insightful, and mind-expanding book that is based on sound research, in-depth case studies, and practical experience. It's a breakthrough work with a unique perspective that will make you think differently about how you think. And, you'll want to return to it regularly for its wise counsel on what you can do to have more of the brilliant and less of the blunder. I highly recommend it."
—Jim Kouzes, coauthor of The Leadership Challenge, and the Dean's Executive Fellow of Leadership, Leavey School of Business, Santa Clara University

"In this marvelous and timely book, Dr. Lippitt helps leaders navigate today's volatile, uncertain, complex, and ambiguous operating environment with a framework creative enough to represent this complicated reality yet practical enough to guide them through it."
—Rob Kaiser, president of Kaiser Leadership Solutions and author of *The Leadership Versatility Index*

"Mary Lippitt's book busts some myths about leadership paradigms. She vividly explains with brilliant examples how mindsets and thought processes add up to much more for decision makers."
—Jaynie L. Smith, CEO, Smart Advantage and Author of *Creating Competitive Advantage*

"This is a well written and seminal work with abundant examples on how to sharpen leadership mindset mastery in real situations faced by businesses and organizations. The wise leader will master the concepts

presented in this book and make sure that leaders in their organization master it as well."
—William D. Anton, Ph.D., Founder of CEOeffectiveness.com and author of *Business Success Through Self-Knowledge*

"Brilliant or Blunder is a well-written and well analyzed study offering new approaches and insights in how leaders can excel in uncertain times."
—Kimo Kippen, Chief Learning Officer, Hilton Worldwide University

"Brilliant or Blunder presents a unique and encompassing approach to leadership and achieving excellence. Insightful, comprehensive and yet very practical."
—Jerry W. Koehler, Faculty Director, MBA Program and Professor of Management and Organization, University of South Florida

"Timely, relevant, practical and oh-so-needed! ... A practical, eye-opening read for leaders at any level and at any tenure in their leadership career."
—Rosario (Ria) Hawkins, Ph.D, President of Take Charge Consulting

"Brilliant or Blunder targets today's critical leadership dilemma—how to handle thorny problems, complexity and risk. Whether you are a new or experienced leader, this book reveals no-nonsense insights on how to develop wise and agile leaders."
—Daniel J. Doyle, Chief Human Resources Officer, Beall's, Inc.

"Brilliant or Blunder deftly takes us on a journey beyond the previous leadership frameworks to a more useful and comprehensive approach. Correctly focused on the decision- making role of leaders, this book changes our leadership mindset in order to help us make better decisions."
—David Marquet, best selling author of *Turn Your Ship Around*

"Brilliant or Blunder provides an excellent roadmap that shows leaders the best ways to handle business changes and avoid falling into old habits of thinking and action. This is not only a book for leaders but also

for entrepreneurs—those operating within organizations as well as those creating new ones."
—David Obstfeld, Associate Professor of Management, California State University Fullerton

"Having worked with the principles and practices presented in *Brilliant or Blunder*, I know that people get it and put these tools to immediate use to benefit themselves and their organizations."
—Don Swartz, chairman and founder, International Institute for The Study of Systems Renewal

"Mary Lippitt's *Brilliant or Blunder* does an excellent job of codifying a business approach to a practical decision-making process that allows a manager to quickly look at things from different perspectives ... Excellent job, Mary!"
—David R Hersey, President, Summit Logistics and Founder, Agile Innovations Solutions.

"Brilliant leadership means getting results ... Delve into this book; it is a must-read from a thought leader who has devoted her career to helping others learn to lead and achieve results. Mary Lippitt's new book, *Brilliant or Blunder*, is—in a word—*brilliant!*"
—Elaine Biech, author *The Business of Consulting*, editor *The ASTD Leadership Handbook and founder of ebb associates inc.*

"In *Brilliant or Blunder*, Mary Lippitt has given us not only a new path to leadership, but a compelling call to change the very way we think."
—Hile Rutledge, President, OKA (Otto Kroeger Associates)

"A clear-eyed look at an aspect of leadership not usually focused upon: mindset ... With lots of great examples and straightforward means for cultivating and using leadership mindsets, this book will help leaders 'slow down to go fast' in our increasingly speeded up world."
—Ethan Schutz, President & CEO, The Schutz Company

BRILLIANT OR
BLUNDER

Brilliant

or

Blunder

6

WAYS LEADERS NAVIGATE UNCERTAINTY, OPPORTUNITY AND COMPLEXITY

Mary B. Lippitt

Enterprise Management
Palm Harbor, Florida

Published by Enterprise Management Ltd. 4531 Roanoak Way, Palm Harbor, FL 34685

Printed in the United States of American.
ISBN 978-0-9715907-5-5

To Sam and Matthew and the other leaders whose brilliant actions will guide us in the future.

Contents

Acknowledgements

My appreciation goes to the many creative minds (both those with and without the Lippitt name) that have thought deeply in leadership, organization development, strategy, and decision science. I have benefited from leaders such as Gordon Lippitt, Ron Lippitt, Jerry Harvey, Daniel Kahneman, Warren Schmidt, Don Swartz, and Peter Vaill.

I am delighted to give special recognition and appreciation to my editor Mark Vickers. He offered a wealth of indispensable editorial advice, steady support and a sharp critical eye. His keen insights disciplined and guided the writing. It is a delight to work with him. His mastery of transforming mental ramblings into readable material was amazing.

Special thanks go to reviewers including Marilyn Billitari, Julie Taubman, Erika Thompson, Anne Rarich, Constance Ridgway, Ron Fleisher, and John Dufresne. The book benefited from their wisdom. Many thanks also to Sara Berglund for her wonderful cover art.

Consulting and coaching clients, program participants, and graduate students are too numerous to mention, but they should be assured that I am deeply indebted to them. Special thanks goes to those who contributed by granting interviews and sharing their experience. This book insufficiently captures their impressive wealth of experience.

Introduction

———

In a career that has spanned thirty years, I have found myself repeatedly encountering the same stumbling blocks in organizations. These can be summed up as inattention to mastering the current context and viewing things from a personal perspective, resulting in a "we/they" outlook. These conflicts cause dysfunction, continually sapping cohesion and performance.

As a result, I have often needed to help defuse executive-team clashes, resolve labor-management disputes, neutralize turf battles, and resuscitate change initiatives. Over and over, I find that when differences are framed in personal terms, participants develop entrenched viewpoints which assume they must "win" because there is only one "right solution" to any given problem.

That's the bad news.

The good news is that these problems can be easily avoided if we incorporate a new type of mindset model into our understanding of leadership. The current view of what constitutes great leadership is too narrow. We tend to believe that a leader's style or expertise defines his or her greatness. Therefore, we imitate the styles of Steve Jobs and Jack Welch in the hope that we can duplicate their brilliant results.

Unfortunately, this gets things backward. Leadership is not about style, traits, or tactics. As the late, great Peter Drucker said, "Leadership is about results."

This book shows us how we can improve our chances of getting better results. The goal is to make more brilliant decisions while avoiding dysfunction-causing blunders. I define brilliance as decisions based on a comprehensive understanding of current reality, an openness to all perspectives, due diligence in analyzing options, and the attainment of the kind of support that leads to smooth implementation. Blunders are those decisions that are flawed from the start because they blindly overlook significant facets.

What I am proposing is adopting a more robust understanding of leadership. In coaching and consulting with thousands of leaders, I have found that many operate based on two concepts. First, they believe that great leadership equates to crafting and gaining support for their vision or goal. Second, they assume that personality and leadership style underlie their ability to implement the announced vision.

Although both concepts have some merit, they are hopelessly incomplete. These approaches omit such crucial issues as ineffective analysis of the situation, weak planning, poor change readiness, weakly articulated benefits, mistaken assumptions, ineffective decision processes, and feeble communication plans. These omissions increase our susceptibility to misunderstandings and miscalculations because they permit us to jump into action hoping for quick fixes or silver bullets.

Brilliance cannot be achieved by shooting blindly in the dark, depending on engrained habits, or merely imitating successful CEOs. In a world of complex challenges and great uncertainties, we must recognize that leadership is too complex for inflexible convictions, knee jerk responses, and simple mandates.

As you can tell, I am very passionate about these subjects. I came by such passion early on as I began discussing leadership and management issues in my teens with my father, Gordon Lippitt. He authored a seminal Harvard Business Review article with Warren Schmidt in 1967; even today that article still provides me with rich insights into the impact of the organizational life cycle and leadership crises points. By combining their expertise along with the contributions of my uncle Ron Lippitt, and other leadership experts, I've come to recognize that leadership practices differ between those who produce brilliant solutions and those who derail progress because of blundering delusions.

Aside from business results, what are the key distinctions between successful and unsuccessful leaders? The two most important ones are (1) brilliant leaders take a comprehensive view of leadership that includes integrating multiple leadership schools of thought and (2) they search for a comprehensive understanding of what matters most right now. Let me expand on these two factors.

BROADENING OUR LEADERSHIP MODELS

Too often we are tempted to try to find one leadership paradigm and apply it in every situation. We want leadership to be simple, even though it is not. I find it essential to take a more inclusive approach that integrates four of the five paradigms or schools of leadership. Let's reflect on the historic schools of leadership.

Table One: Leadership Paradigms

Time Period	Dominant Leadership Paradigm	Examples
Pre-Industrial Era	Inherited (firstborn male; ruling class)	Crown prince, Son of tribal chief, Aristocracy
Industrial Era	Personal characteristics or "Great Man" theory	Decisiveness, Integrity, Work ethic, Commanding presence, Loyalty, Courage, Honor, Self-awareness
Modern Era, 1940-1980	Leadership style of working with others	Participative, Autocratic, Laissez-faire, Teaming, Situational leadership
Information Era, 1980-2000	Leadership skills and competencies	Strategic planning, Financial monitoring, Delegating, Coaching, Presentation skills, Emotional intelligence
Global Era, 2000 to present	Effectiveness, context-based action and agility	Mindset and priority balance, Organizational life cycle alignment, Systems thinking, Due diligence, Engagement

Leadership would be easier if one of these models sufficed. Unfortunately, none can cope with the difficult challenges facing us today. If they did, leadership would be easy rather than the perplexing conundrum that it is. Given the fact that the track record for successful change initiatives remains about thirty percent and we have greater executive turnover than ever before, it is time to rethink our assumptions and expand our practices.

We certainly have made progress over the centuries. We no longer think that leadership is an inherited gene, gender, or class. We have also advanced from the assumption that individual characteristics such as charisma, integrity, or decisiveness alone predict leadership performance. We now know that less charismatic leaders have often succeeded where more mesmerizing individuals failed.

The leadership school that targeted style (what I've labeled the Modern Era in Table One) examines how leaders should interact with others, assign work, lead teams, and balance responsibilities. This is helpful but does not guarantee successful outcomes. We all know people who are wonderful to be with but achieve very little. A fuller picture is needed.

Disappointment with a reliance on style alone led to a new emphasis on knowledge and skills. Yet, this competency-based strategy, like the previous style-based strategy, is relatively stable, leading only to the kind of gradual improvement which is inadequate for today's fast pace. Competencies are important, but research shows it is the effective application of competencies that counts. Knowledge alone does not equate to great leaders. If it did, businesses would recruit their CEOs from universities, and we know that does not happen very often. While some leaders move easily from one industry or field to another without industry-specific knowledge, others who have spent their entire lives in one field falter. It isn't what you know but what you do with your knowledge that defines great leaders.

That brings us to what I've deemed the "Global Era" in Table One where the emphasis of the leadership centers on achieving the best results given the current situation. It entails identifying current circumstances, systems thinking, comprehensive analysis, and agility. But even this leadership model must be integrated with three of the older models for sustained excellence.

By melding traits, styles, and competencies with context mastery we can truly be effective. Since much has been written about the first three schools, this book will explore the context mastery and agility approach, which gives us a greater chance of making brilliant decisions by employing six mindsets.

Leadership mindsets avoid the kinds of dysfunctional conflicts and flawed initiatives mentioned above because it offers a non-individual aspect and increases our flexibility when navigating new realities. It also helps us remain alert to change, accurately grasp complex issues, analyze potential ramifications, and capture opportunities.

The illustration below captures how the four schools of leadership overlap to form a new leadership "sweet spot." My focus in this book centers on the mindset framework, since much has been written on style, character, and skills.

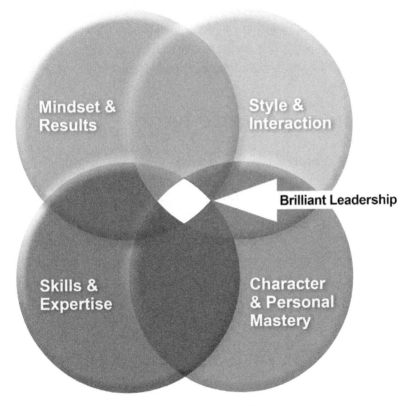

Figure One: The Source of Brilliant Leadership

This framework enables us to deal with these pressing questions:

- What is the best course of action at this juncture?
- What can I do to rapidly develop capacity in others?
- How do I encourage agility to effectively manage uncertain and complex issues?
- How do I align organizational energies for goal achievement?
- How do I develop an adaptive and change-ready culture?

A flexible and vibrant leadership framework is needed to cope with uncertainty and complexity. The mindset model adds a dynamic dimension to the other three more stable schools. And this perspective can be quickly learned and applied. Instead of offering a specific decision-making process or an update on neuroscience, this book offers six frames of reference for analyzing realities to select a sound path toward maximizing opportunities and mitigating risk.

ENHANCING OUR PERSPECTIVES

Mindsets largely determine how we view the world. We frequently have become too comfortable with one lens or mindset based on past experience. A limited or myopic perspective blinds us to potentially significant trends and realities.

Operating from only one mindset, we are tempted to jump into action even when a situation is complex, precedent-setting, or highly consequential. Of course, we all *think* we don't do this, but we tend to fool ourselves. As a quick illustration, please count the number of times the letter F appears in the following:

FINISHED FILES ARE THE RESULT OF YEARS OF SCIENTIFIC STUDY COMBINED WITH THE EXPERIENCE OF MANY YEARS

Most of us, including a group of newspaper editors, count three, but there are six. We ignore the Fs in the words "of," which appears three times. We skip over them since they're "not important." When we skip over "insignificant" aspects or when we rely too heavily on past patterns, we operate from a blind spot that may lead to a costly blunder.

Confronting uncertainties means that we cannot skip over "minor" elements. We must decipher the whole picture before leaping into action. After all, the "ready, fire" technique is particularly dangerous when mistakes can threaten an organization's survival or a leader's career. Brilliant outcomes stem from the practice of "ready, *aim*, fire." The question is, how do we ensure that our aim is true? Since we cannot rely on old data, past patterns, or wishful thinking, we need a new framework to ensure a full understanding of options and risks.

The old admonition of keeping your eyes on the prize assumes that we must adopt a singular focus. This will not work when we deal with increasing uncertainty. The mindset framework covers six mental lenses or action viewpoints for a holistic understanding of our current context. The mindsets are: 1) developing new products or services, 2) gaining and satisfying customers, 3) building an effective infrastructure, 4) increasing efficiencies, 5) developing a high-performance culture, and 6) positioning for the future.

Organizations are continually shifting, and these shifts present new opportunities, fresh risks and new challenges. We all know that businesses crash if they assume a current fad is permanent; fast-rising startups fizzle if they fail to create financial controls; mature firms shrivel if they are lulled into accepting complacency; and organizations striving for renewal blunder if they embark recklessly on unsuitable mergers.

Brilliant or Blunder offers leaders a new model to, first, analyze their current reality and then, second, to increase agility by sharing and using the mindset framework with others. I hope you will find this a practical and flexible leadership framework.

USING THE BOOK

There are three sections in *Brilliant or Blunder.* In *Part One, A New Leadership Framework,* Chapter 1 examines thinking patterns, presents the value of a mindset framework and offers a short inventory to gauge your current mindset. Chapter 2 focuses on the mindset framework, explains how to interpret the assessment, describes the organizational life cycle and encourages you to continually scan and adjust to changing internal and external realities.

Part Two, Expanding Mindset Agility, describes each mindset and how it deciphers current and changing context. Chapters 3 through 8 describe what each mindset is seeking, how it contributes to effective leadership, and its potential liabilities if used to excess. Because each mindset has a unique approach to analyzing the context, knowing how to recognize each is key to improving communication, aligning efforts, and engaging others to achieve goals. These chapters include anecdotes of leaders operating from each priority, illustrative situations, and case studies. I would like to note that these case examples describe an aspect of an organization at a moment in time and do not imply that past examples represent current mindsets.

Chapters 9 and 10 constitute the final section, *Leveraging the Power of Mindsets,* which discusses how to apply mindsets to conflict management, gaining greater influence and team alignment. Chapter 9 explains how the context-based approach handles conflict and how to gain active support for implementation. A chart describing how to predict the priorities, as well as the recommended strategies for establishing mutually satisfying results, enables you to quickly apply this process.

Chapter 10 examines how teams can use mindsets to ensure effective and aligned decisions. It outlines how to analyze team strengths and avoid potential blind spots.

In summary, this book argues that brilliant action stems from an integrated leadership approach that includes the use of mindsets to analyze the current context and reveal wiser choices in order to cope with the daunting challenges facing us today.

GOALS AND CONTRIBUTIONS

The goal of the book is to encourage a pragmatic, tailored, and comprehensive approach that can be used to assist current leaders and develop future leaders. My research with more than 6,000 leaders provides quantified findings, anecdotal evidence supporting the mindset framework, and a reliable and validated inventory for recognizing individual and team priorities. After all, leadership is a constant balancing act.

It is my hope that this book encourages greater engagement and interest in discovering alternatives to ensure the results we get are the results that we want.

ONE

A New
Leadership Framework

—

Getting Leadership Right

My great concern is not whether you have failed,
but whether you are content with your failure.

–Abraham Lincoln

Adapting action to meet new challenges is the
definition of intelligence.

—Unknown

In the business world, the rearview mirror is
always clearer than the windshield.

–Warren Buffett

Leadership has been dissected, inflated, lionized, and trivialized. However, the
essence remains the same: the leader's key role is to get things done, make wise
decisions, launch effective plans, and mobilize others to implement plans. They
accomplish this by being acutely aware of their environment. They do *not* act in
a vacuum or assume that what has happened in the past is all that can happen in
the future. They are proactive, future-focused, and flexible.

Unfortunately, this is the ideal rather than the reality. Common practice is often quite different. Leaders make brilliant decisions sometimes, but other times they stumble, flounder, or miscalculate. A blunder comes from flawed thinking at the start, not the result of bad luck.

Why does this happen? Because leaders tend to be like everyone else: that is, their thinking is constrained. When most of us make decisions, about eighty percent of the time we choose about twenty percent of the choices available to us. This dynamic is known as the Pareto Principle, and it tends to influence how we approach challenging situations. If we look at our closets, we will tend to wear twenty percent of our clothes. If we look at wear patterns on our rugs at home, they are about twenty percent of the potential area.

Such tendencies are sometimes useful. Even in business, they can help us focus on what is most important, such as the twenty percent of customers who account for eighty percent of sales.

However, we can also become the victims of our own patterns of thought, *especially* if we are business leaders. Research by Dr. Paul Nutt at Ohio State suggests that eighty percent of the time executives do not consider an alternative before making a decision. Instead, they rely on the "tried-and-true" responses they have used in the past.

This is a dangerous tendency when our organizations confront fast-changing and uncertain environments. It accounts for many of the business mistakes and failures we have seen in recent decades.

Research increasingly shows that leaders who engage in more comprehensive analyses gain leverage in the marketplace and reduce the chances of major blunders. Such leaders become more agile, make smarter decisions, and are better able to gain the support of others.

Improving one's analytical skills is not rocket science. It is easy to learn and practice. We can become considerably more effective by using a mindset framework that is tailored to our unique situations. In this book, we will examine six mindsets and describe how leaders can select the most appropriate mindset as their current driving priority in order to capture opportunities and resolve problems.

BRILLIANT LEADERSHIP IN ACTION

To illustrate how analytical thinking produces brilliant outcomes, let us examine someone confronted with a major crisis. In August of 2010, 33 miners in Chile were caught in a massive cave-in, trapping them 2,300 feet underground in the San Jose copper mine. It was an unprecedented and horrific accident. No standard rescue was possible.

Laurence Golborne had recently become the Chilean Mining Minister, stepping in as part of a newly elected government four months earlier. He had no background in mining, though he had proven himself an astute chief executive officer at Cencosud S.A., a large retail firm. Suddenly, he was required to lead "one of the most widely watched disaster recovery efforts in world history," according to a case study from the Wharton School at the University of Pennsylvania.

Without warning, Golborne was thrust into making life or death decisions. He knew that knee-jerk decisions could get people killed. He opted for comprehensive analysis, collaboration with mining and rescue experts, and a commitment to transparency that yielded a carefully orchestrated process.

This is not to say that he did not act decisively. In most crisis situations, some decisions must be made quickly. Golborne made two important decisions in short order. First, he decided to go to the mine personally. Politically speaking, this was dangerous. By becoming closely affiliated with a crisis that might end in disaster, he risked becoming permanently linked with the eventual outcomes, potentially damaging his government's reputation.

His second quick decision was made during an initial meeting attended by diverse interests: A local government official, police officers, rescue team leaders, a top military officer in the region, a local representative of Chile's National Emergency Office, and one of the owners of the mine. During that meeting, which was characterized by confusion and uncertainty, Golborne decided to lead the whole rescue effort.

Even as he took charge, however, Golborne recognized his limitations. He stated, "I do not have technical knowledge, [but] what I do know is how to manage challenging projects, lead people, build teams, and provide the necessary resources." Among his top priorities were:

[5]

- *Transparent communication.* He told the relatives of the trapped miners that they would receive honest news of the situation. He made sure they were informed every two hours of what was happening.

- *Team building and engagement.* He ensured that the right people were involved in the decision-making process. He defined his job as a facilitator and resource provider.

- *Coordinating and consulting.* In the end, experts from the Chilean Navy, NASA, and multi-national mining firms representing Latin America, South Africa, Australia, U.S., and Canada were consulted.

- *Asking the right questions and listening to experts.* His goal was to ask the kinds of questions that would enable wise decisions. He said, "I started asking questions. Why are you putting in this winch? What alternatives are there?" He also carefully listened to others, extracting key concerns and alternatives.

- *Delegating.* He ensured that there were experts and leaders accountable for different aspects of the rescue, including working with the families of the miners, leading the technical team, and taking charge of the medical conditions of the miners. For example, the leader responsible for medical conditions made sure the miners would receive not only healthcare assistance but psychological and dietary aid. It was important that the miners be fit enough to enter the small capsule that would eventually take them to the surface, requiring some of the trapped miners to slim down. These were the types of combined efforts that made the rescue a success.

- *Managing expectations.* He did not allow expectations of success to quickly escalate. He knew many things could go wrong and he communicated honestly with the media, sometimes taking short-term hits to his own public image.

When it was discovered that the miners were alive, ten different methods were identified to bring them to the surface. Eventually three methods were deemed most likely to succeed. Plan A involved drilling a shaft down directly to the miners. Plan B involved widening the boreholes that had been drilled in an effort to locate and communicate with the miners. Place C entailed using a petroleum rig to dig a hole.

Golborne was responsible for communicating the options to Chile's President Piñera, who later stated, "Minister Laurence Golborne informed me that there were three technological options for the rescue and asked me to define which one we would use. I told him [all] three of them because technologies may fail, but we cannot fail."

In the end, it proved to be a wise decision. As the Wharton case study notes, "At the moment when the rescue shaft under Plan B had reached the miners at 700 meters below the surface, the shaft under Plan A had reached only 598 meters, and the shaft under Plan C had reached just 372 meters." Ultimately, the miners were brought to the surface 69 days after the cave-in, much earlier than the original four month timeframe.

Golborne was not the only leader during the crisis. President Piñera made crucial decisions, as did many of the people responsible for different parts of the rescue. But Golborne's actions illustrate some critical leadership mindsets that we will explore throughout this book:

- An ability to recognize that there were unknowns that required a deeper dive into the situation.
- A willingness to act decisively when necessary, while knowing when to take the proper amount of time and care to evaluate complex situations.
- A readiness to consult and work with others.
- A desire and ability to ask good and revealing questions.
- An ability to seek out and carefully consider various points of view.
- A willingness to monitor, adjust, and reprioritize based on new information or changing circumstances.

- An agility that stems from keeping an open mind about which strategies and tactics may prove to be most effective.
- An ability to gain respect and support from followers who have been consulted and who have a clear idea of why and how certain decisions have been made.

Golborne's leadership was not only displayed by what he did but by what he *didn't* do. He did not succumb to various decision-making traps that so often hinder leader effectiveness and spawn missteps.

He did not become wedded to one perspective based on habit or history. His desire to search for alternatives and entertain multiple rescue scenarios reflected an open mind.

Although he did make some preliminary decisions quickly, he did not make snap decisions driven by his pride, his authority, or his fears. Therefore, he honestly considered options, examined facts, or listened to multiple points of view.

He did not fall into the trap of "rapid pattern recognition" in which leaders erroneously apply past blueprints to new situations. Too often, just as star watchers look at the night sky and search for the Big Dipper because it is an easily recognized pattern, leaders selectively search for information that conforms to old patterns, thereby filtering out data that does not seem to fit. In this way, they often miss key factors.

He did not engage in an unrealistically "can do" attitude. He was willing to communicate frank assessments and even bad news. While there were times he sought to balance out unduly negative points of view, he did not coerce others to "get on board" and thereby foster group think. Positive thinking is constructive during a plan's execution, but all the facts must be understood and incorporated into the plan before execution starts. Simply wishing or wanting success cannot make it real.

He did not stumble into the experience trap. In this case, it is possible that his lack of experience in the mining industry actually helped him encourage creative thinking. Falling into an experience trap happens when leaders buy into the illusion that simplicity and speed equate with superlative solutions. Leaders may think there is no need to explore all viewpoints based on the false assumption that everything is known and on the table.

He did not abdicate responsibility. He relied on experts but continued to serve as a primary leader, guiding and coordinating processes as the situation evolved.

He did not assume he could engage in extreme multitasking to handle all facets of the rescue. He delegated when necessary and found experts who possessed greater knowledge than he had. Too many leaders assume they should be able to read a report, make a decision, and hold a conversation on different matters all at the same time in the name of efficiency and time management. The truth is, no one can. Handling dissimilar details pushes our brains—both young and old—beyond our ability. We are all limited to keeping five to seven things in our short term memory, and most of today's decisions go far beyond that number.

BLUNDERS AND BLIND SPOTS

Not every leader demonstrates such wisdom or produces brilliantly conceived plans. Some leaders fall victim to the fallacy that there is no time to be indecisive, no time to think, and no time to confer with others. The problem is not bad luck or poor timing but ineffective analysis. Blunders are flawed from the start. We must take the time to get it right the first time, since some decisions are permanent and cannot be reversed.

Consider the 2003 United States decision to invade Iraq based on the assumption that weapons of mass destruction (WMD) were being held by Iraqi leader Saddam Hussein. It was a matter of historic record that Hussein had used chemical weapons on his own people in the 1980s. When, in the aftermath of the 9/11 terrorist attacks, one informant reported that Hussein was still harboring WMD, the information was deemed credible despite the fact that United Nations weapons inspectors could find no such stockpiles. The U.S. government subsequently authorized the Iraq War based on the expectation that there were WMD in Iraq. Today, we know that the informant was unreliable and that WMD were never found.

Such blunders are not limited to the political realm. In 2001, the bursting of the telecom bubble resulted in the loss of two trillion dollars in market value, largely from laying more fiber optic cable than was needed. This mistake proves that if you build it, they will not always come. Internet use, video on demand, and entertainment downloads were growing, but traffic was not doubling every three months as some anticipated. Given an industry debt load estimated at $650 billion, it is not surprising that many firms went bankrupt or were acquired.

Telecoms are not the only companies sometimes operating with false assumptions and making faulty decisions. Leaders at retail giant Target Corporation, for example, decided to rapidly expand into Canada, where it eventually lost nearly a billion dollars. These losses, combined with a 2013 security breach that affected forty million customers, resulted in the dismissal of both the CEO and the CIO.

The U.S. (and eventually global) financial crisis in 2009 also stemmed from industry-wide miscalculations. Weak internal controls enabled some traders to exceed their authority in placing risky trades. There was also widespread misrepresentation of the real value of some investments. And, of course, there were the problems in the mortgage industry, which assumed that it was safe to offer loans up to 95% of the home's value based on the assumption that home prices never fall more than five percent. Home owners can now attest to the fact that home prices can fall dramatically more than five percent, which drastically affected home owners, banks, and the world's economy.

CULTIVATING BRILLIANCE

Brilliant decisions are made independent of personal intelligence or experience. Many talented leaders falter because of overconfidence in their astute thinking or a belief in their invulnerability. By themselves, individuals are rarely capable of gathering and analyzing all the information associated with today's complex systems. To be brilliant while avoiding blunders, we must augment our "gut feelings" with in-depth and comprehensive analyses. We also need a practical framework to ensure that we understand all relevant factors before we leap into action.

Going with our first impressions or a "sixth sense" can be beneficial when we are dealing with familiar situations. However, research suggests that such gut feelings can also mislead us. To get a practical idea of how this works, quickly answer the following questions:

1. How many animals of any species did Moses take on his ark?
2. If it takes 5 machines 5 minutes to make 5 widgets, how long would it take 100 machines to make 100 widgets? 100 minutes or 5 minutes?
3. Which is longer: the table on the right or the one the left?

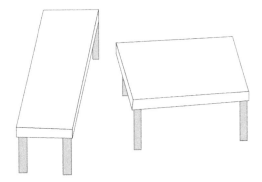

4. How many faces are in the picture below?

If you're like most people, you answered each question with the obvious response. However, if you had taken time to engage in more analytical thinking, you would likely have arrived at different conclusions. For example, most of us know that two of each species were on the ark, so our immediate answer is two. Yet, we recognize, with some more thought, that Noah rather than Moses built the ark.

We tend to solve the first problem we see without considering the whole context. In the second question, our gut reaction is that it would take 100 minutes. This response might have been encouraged because 100 was the first potential answer. With a little more scrutiny, we realize that it would take the same five minutes.

Perception also influences and channels our thinking and responses. Sometimes our eyes deceive us, particularly when two items are displayed at different angles. The tables depicted in the third example are the same size, but our depth perception makes this conclusion hard to accept. (Since most of us find it impossible to believe that they are the same, use a ruler to prove it to yourself.)

Perception and a tendency to settle for a "good enough" response misdirect us in the fourth question. The average number of faces cited is three: the face of the old man, the face of the young woman, and the face of the peasant whose hat is formed by the old man's eyebrow with the old man's nose becoming the peasant's arm. However, there are four others: the baby's face, the profile formed by the urn with the bird perched on top, the full face formed to the left of that urn, and the profile of the woman formed by that urn on the right.

When we identify a solution, we may think our job is done. However, stopping at an initial solution may produce a less optimum or great solution. We need to take the time to strive for the best response when the organization faces uncertainty and complexity.

These questions illustrate that we (1) tend to focus on the main question asked rather than examine and evaluate all of the facts, (2) feel that we can simultaneously collect and evaluate complex data accurately, (3) over rely on the notion that we see all there is to see, and (4) often stop thinking about a question when we have a "good enough" response, believing we have done our job—even when we haven't found the optimal answer.

Tapping Two Thinking Systems

The exercises above are designed to give you insights into two systems of thinking. In his book *Thinking, Fast and Slow* (2011), Nobel Prize winner Daniel Kahneman refers to these two approaches in the following ways:

Fast Thinking: Automatic, emotional, intuitive, natural, impulsive, focused, implicit, reactive, spontaneous, single minded, narrow

Slow Thinking: Analytical, calculating, reasoned, challenging, abstract, explicit, systematic, expansive, exploratory, comprehensive

Kahneman suggests that when we need to make wise decisions to respond to complex issues, we should use "slow thinking," even though it takes greater concentration, effort, and time. The benefit is that we get it right the first time. Sometimes, even seemingly simple questions (such as those above) require more analysis than we initially assumed. Resistance to slow thinking frequently (and naturally) stems from the fact that it is perceived as taking too long. Yet fixing a blunder often takes a great deal more time and energy. The best course is to guarantee that the first call is the right one.

Slow thinking tends to be more important as we tackle complicated issues, changing realities, additional regulations, newer technologies, and even more demanding customers. However, successfully using this type of thinking cannot be equated with just a simple message that we should slow down and look at the issue more carefully. Our thinking has to include a comprehensive understanding of the current context.

Why? One reason is stress, which is endemic in today's business world. Research by Richard Boyatzis and others find that stress and the sense of urgency impact our thinking. When we are stressed, our brain activity tends to be focused in the action-oriented parts of our brain, rather than in parts associated with creative and analytical thinking.

In fact, when we assume we have limited time, we encounter stress, anxiety, or fear that often prevents us from fully grasping all facets or considering innovative alternatives. One way to handle this is to acknowledge that we create this stress for ourselves and that the real goal is not speed but

[13]

brilliant results. Therefore, we should step back, reduce rush to judgment, and grant ourselves the freedom to conduct a broad and deep analysis. Only when we can see the whole picture, understand the risk, and know how to prepare for consequences can we make exceptional choices.

These tactics, however, assume that we have a framework or model that enables us to comprehend and analyze complex situations. We need templates or models to help us organize our thinking, understand systems and recognize connections. Recall your high-school chemistry class with its famous depiction of the periodic table of elements on the wall. While we may have struggled with it, we also benefited from it, since it provided us with a systematic way to analyze relationships and connections between the elements.

The medical community also uses models and diagnostic checklists to guarantee a complete understanding of their patients' maladies. In addition, hospital checklists and reference materials such as the *Physicians' Desk Reference* and the *Diagnostic and Statistical Manual of Mental Disorders* alert medical professionals to potential interactions, risks, and alternatives. Physicians do not "wing it," and leaders shouldn't either.

As leaders, we need a good framework that allows us to balance first impressions with a comprehensive situational analysis. In addition, a worthwhile framework will help us communicate effectively with those who are involved and those who will be impacted. As Golborne demonstrated in Chile, great outcomes surface when problems are carefully scrutinized, when there is a diligent search for the best solution, and when the process, parameters and criteria are communicated. One of the primary goals of this book is to provide you with a framework that helps you find and implement brilliant decisions.

HARNESSING MINDSETS

Many leaders rely on internal models, but even if those models are inclusive and effective, they tend to have limited benefit. They are likely poorly understood by others. A model must be widely understood so it can be consistently applied across an organization. Without common application, our ability to uncover information, analyze options, and creatively identify new solutions is limited.

We need a collective framework to maximize our ability to get the right solution in each circumstance and to ensure that others actively support the decision.

The "mindset" framework in this book is one that can be easily mastered, shared, and utilized. A mindset is a mental lens to collect, evaluate, and respond to challenges confronting us. Everyone has a mindset, which can also be called a viewpoint, point of view, outlook, assumption, perspective, priority or frame of reference. Mindsets determine what we buy, what we do, and what we resist.

Consider the decision to purchase a car. A buyer with a "safety first" mindset might be attracted to one car model, a buyer who prioritizes luxury and status might be attracted to another. Other mindsets prioritize aspects such as fuel economy, resale value, seating capacity, insurance costs, or horsepower. All these mindsets are "correct," but each specific buyer will value some more than others based on their perception of their particular needs and preferences.

Frequently, though, our wants or needs conflict with each another. For example, we may have established the top price we want to pay but then find out that for *only* a few hundred dollars more we can get more miles per gallon. Then we must decide which mindset is our highest priority. If price is paramount, we may calculate whether higher gas mileage will saves us enough money over the car's lifetime to justify a higher initial cost.

At work, our mindset influences how we see, interpret, and act on opportunities and problems. And just as in the decision to buy a car, it can be difficult to make the trade-offs between mindsets. After all, few of us can get what we want when we want it for the price we want. We feel torn between alternatives. Careful consideration must be given to which mindset and outcome we want to achieve first at this moment in time.

Some leaders, for example, ask others to work "faster, cheaper and better." Most of us recognize the inherent conflict in that directive. We know when we reduce costs, there is often a negative impact on quality or speed. If our attention focuses on making things more quickly, cost goes up due to increased staffing, equipment usage, overtime, or increased maintenance. There really is no free lunch, even though we wish there were. Everything has a price. There may be a creative way to meet such requests, but even that requires time and talent to investigate. Fully analyzing a situation may seem like an unnecessary delay. And leaders may fear a lack of action will be interpreted as waffling. However, when analysis precedes, we improve outcomes and gain support.

A template or framework ensures that we make smart trade-offs and wise decisions. Otherwise, like someone who purchases the wrong car, we experience a kind of "buyer's remorse" when we recognize that our decisions were made without full analysis of the alternatives and the outcome is less than desired.

Staying Agile and Relevant

Mindsets are dynamic and need to change as circumstances shift. The rate of changes is accelerating and so are opportunities. We cannot count on equilibrium externally or internally. Our mindsets must be agile enough to navigate this change and allow our organizations to survive and thrive.

The need to respond to change sounds like common sense. Yet, most of us still regularly stumble into the kinds of perception traps that cause us to get stuck grasping to one mindset. This is treacherous for business leaders; organizations that fail to adapt to change become the proverbial buggy whip manufacturer—with a long history and a short future.

When one specific mindset is selected as the critical framework for handling the current situation, it is called a "priority" or a "driving" mindset. Leaders' priorities reflect their current thinking, decision-making criteria, and goals. Leaders who continually scan the environment are able to reprioritize their thinking and produce higher quality decisions.

For instance, a leader might focus on increasing market share by 5% and, when that is achieved, the priority might change to restructuring the organization to cope with the expanding customer base. After that is completed, a new priority around quality improvement might become the focus. There are always new ways to excel and new opportunities to leverage.

Even after we have selected a priority, we must continually monitor the others to remain appropriately on target. This means we have to constantly scan the business environment for new information and evolving trends. When the situation shifts significantly, a new mindset might need to take precedence.

Gaining acceptance and support from others also requires an agile mindset. We must see the situation or challenge from another individual's, unit's, or profession's viewpoint. Understanding another's frame of reference permits us to speak to their interests and stress the benefits that they seek.

Instead of seeing agility as an impediment that detracts from a "steady as she goes" course, it is an advantage. Operating from multiple mindsets uncovers new solutions, increases engagement, avoids blind spots, and results in wiser decisions.

Detecting Business Mindsets

In the workplace, there are six basic mindsets—or frames of reference—that tend to drive decision-making. In the following chapters, this book will describe these mindsets, show how they connect with one another, highlight how they can be used, and how you can detect which ones are currently driving decisions and actions.

Understanding these mindsets does not require an advanced degree, years of experience, psychological assessments, or a personality transplant. It *does* require observation, an open mind, a commitment to excellence and a willingness to ask questions and listen for new ideas.

Questions such as "What is your goal?" or "What is the top priority?" can easily reveal a driving mindset or priority. A less formal request, such as "What is keeping you awake at night?", also provides keen insights that cannot be gained by asking about leadership philosophy or style (In fact, many leaders' description of their management style don't reflect their actual practices.)

We can also observe mindsets in action. Is someone putting customer needs over profit? Are resources being allocated to quality improvement rather than innovation? Is the marketing staff increasing while the engineering budget is being cut? Whatever the choice or action, it reveals which mindset currently drives decision making.

Making these choices is difficult. It is hard to address competing requests with limited resources such as budget, staff, equipment, and facilities. We all want what we currently value the most, even if it means rocking the boat. Helping others appreciate different perspectives encourages a search for common ground. Choices and compromises have to be made in a complicated environment where requests are abundant, many things are uncertain and failure can be devastating.

Rejecting Easy Answers

In a complex world, panaceas or silver bullets are tempting because they appear to offer clarity, commitment, and precision—but they are dangerous. We can easily become infatuated with some all-purpose solution or promising quick fix, while ignoring genuine threats and opportunities. Winston Churchill defined a fanatic as "someone who will not change his mind and will not change the subject." In the business world, fanatics with a "magic wand" solution reduce organizational agility and increase the likelihood of blundering decisions. We have to move beyond an easy answer or the quick fix to using thorough analysis from all points of view.

We also must avoid latching onto the latest fad. New ideas and "best practices" should be analyzed, customized, tested, and evaluated in light of specific needs and requirements. After all, success in one field does not guarantee success in another. Replicating a best practice from another firm often results in disappointment since no two organizations are exactly alike. Context and culture count.

Selecting and monitoring mindsets enable a firm to accurately diagnose and address its unique circumstances and issues. It allows leaders to avoid decision making traps, identify potential barriers to change, and customize solutions to capture and leverage current realities. In addition, the mindset framework unleashes pent-up energy and initiative. Without understanding the current priority, we 1) keep doing what we have always done, 2) wait to see what will happen next, 3) keep our heads down and stay out of trouble. The problem is that staying out of trouble and doing what has been done before means that discretionary effort and innovative thinking are squelched. It is a recipe for becoming outdated and out of touch with customers.

ASSESSING YOUR MINDSET

Far too often, we mistake mindsets and priorities for personality traits, leadership styles, or fixed convictions. That is, we assume "Person Y only cares about X. That's just how he is wired." We may also discount input from some individuals based on their profession or assume that all people in a specific position have the same viewpoint.

Such assumptions do far more harm than good. We must understand that mindsets are situational. They are not "right," "wrong," or permanent. They reflect the lens we are currently using to view the world. A leader's priorities are driven by external (e.g., competitors, regulations, economy, customers) and internal (e.g., management practices, staffing, talent, culture) factors. Our mindset priorities represent our choices about what is most important to accomplish *at this point in time.* They are not engrained or innate. They are more like software than hardware. Just as we use programs, such as Excel or PowerPoint, for different purposes, we adopt different mindset priorities depending on current goals and circumstances. They are the tools we need to get a critical job done.

To get a snapshot of your current driving mindset, review the following three questions from the *Leadership Spectrum Profile®.* Answer all three questions as they relate to one specific current work situation, task, project, or assignment. Remember that there is no right or wrong answer. This is only a short snapshot to help you understand the mindset framework that will be explored in the next chapter.

CURRENT MINDSET EXERCISE

Directions

*Think of a work situation that presents or presented complexity, uncertainty or opportunity. Circle **one** response that best indicates your thinking about what is (or was) the most important alternative to address **first**. Answer all three questions as they relate to your selected work situation.*

1. When a difficult decision needs to be made in regard to this work situation, your inclination is to first:
   A. Generate multiple decision possibilities
   B. Seek agreement from others on the decision you favor
   C. Develop a process or system to generate possible alternatives
   D. Identify potential risks associated with each possible decision
   E. Seek or provide details that will be needed for you or others to conduct a careful analysis
   F. Question current assumptions associated with the situation

2. If you want to convince a peer to accept a specific idea related to this work situation, how are you most likely accomplish this?
   A. Present it as a fresh concept
   B. Demonstrate how it can be mutually beneficial
   C. Present it as logical and attainable, given existing resources
   D. Stress how the idea will result in better performance and meet financial goals
   E. Emphasize how the idea supports existing initiatives and practices
   F. Tie the idea to the "big picture" or current strategy

3. Envision an effectively run enterprise that handles this particular situation well. How would you describe that organization?
   A. Innovative
   B. Customer or market-driven
   C. Organized
   D. Efficient
   E. Consistent
   F. Strategically driven

CURRENT MINDSET EXERCISE

Interpreting the Exercise

Count the number of times you have circled each letter. If all your selections were the same letter, such as "A", you have selected a single mindset. If you have circled more than one letter, you are currently using multiple mindsets in this situation.

Identifying the Mindsets

While each of the six mindsets will be described in separate chapters, the following chart indicates your current mindset for the situation you selected.

YOUR SELECTION

Letter	Mindset
A	Inventing
B	Catalyzing
C	Developing
D	Performing
E	Protecting
F	Challenging

2

The Untethered Mind

There are no old roads to guide us to a new future.

—Unknown

The chains of habit are too light to be felt until they're too heavy to be broken.

—Warren Buffett, quoting Dr. Samuel Johnson

People only see what they are prepared to see.

—Ralph Waldo Emerson

John Dewey, in his 1910 book *How We Think*, pointed to the need for multidimensional thinking to avoid the "natural reaction." He suggested that our first reaction to an event or challenge spontaneously surfaces as a "gut" or default response. Wisdom surfaces after we decide what to add to our early reaction.

An analytical process is critical in discovering novel vantage points to understand new complex situations. At the famously innovative Xerox PARC lab, it was said that "a point of view is worth eighty IQ points."

The fact that we live in a turbulent world makes things even more difficult. Today's careful analysis may no longer be relevant in another few months. Or, as Einstein suggested, "The answers keep changing."

BEFORE MAKING UP OUR MINDS

We are all under pressure to "make up our minds" and take action. However, the pressure for quick action hinders our ability to consider brilliant answers because we revert to basic "fight or flight" impulses. To discover brilliant decisions and plans, we must have a system, framework, or template to ensure that we fully grasp the situation before taking decisive action.

Leaders can use the six mindsets to create a cohesive and systematic picture of current circumstances and alternatives. In many ways, this process parallels how we approach a jigsaw puzzle. We typically start by completing the puzzle's frame, which provides us with clues on how to assemble the remaining interior pieces to produce a complete picture.

Likewise, our initial thoughts about a given situation should serve as a frame for further analysis. It is up to us to find the missing pieces. A mindset framework enables us to fill the vacuum with additional insights and perspectives. When we have the whole picture, we can more easily determine the most pressing issue or our current top priority.

Your responses to the three questions from the *Leadership Spectrum Profile®* at the end of Chapter 1 provide a snapshot of your mindset in one situation. (You are invited to complete the entire inventory online, free, by e-mailing our firm at info@enterprisemgt.com and identifying yourself as a reader.)

Understanding your driving mindset gives you better insight into the factors you are currently emphasizing and those that you may be overlooking. In addition, the mindset framework enables you to craft a compelling message that will appeal to multiple points of view.

Think about your responses to the questions in Chapter 1 and review the mindsets you identified. The following definitions will give you a better understanding of those mindsets.

Inventing

The Inventing Mindset stresses the need for developing new products or services. It promotes change and encourages others to consider new technology, creative alternatives, new synergies, and different methods, rather than relying on the way things have been done in the past.

Catalyzing

The Catalyzing Mindset focuses on customers and strives for fast action to meet customer needs. It values dedicated, aligned, and unified effort to meet market demands and surpass the competition. This priority leverages negotiation and influence to achieve challenging goals.

Developing

The Developing Mindset recognizes the importance of developing a solid organizational framework and infrastructure. This structure provides clear roles and responsibilities to help its users achieve excellence. It also promotes effective reporting relationships, delegation, policy, and seamless systems.

Performing

The Performing Mindset values process improvement in quality, efficiency, effectiveness, and workflow. It strives to refine and upgrade operations, reduce overhead costs, increase cycle time, reduce waste, and improve financial performance.

Protecting

The Protecting Mindset focuses on the organization's culture, developing and retaining talent, and sustaining trust and cooperation. It recognizes the value of existing systems and traditions. It understands how people and morale impact results. The Protecting Mindset also recognizes the importance of succession planning to maintain a high-performing culture.

Challenging

The Challenging Mindset questions assumptions and practices to discover new perspectives and opportunities. It focuses on emerging needs, future opportunities, and learning from experience. This point of view seeks new business models, emerging trends for new product lines, the acceptance of change, and reasonable risk-taking for sustainability.

RESPECTING MINDSET PRIORITIES

Leaders are likely to prioritize just one or two mindsets at a time to concentrate on the important and urgent issues. Of the more than 6,000 leaders who completed the *Leadership Spectrum Profile*, forty-five percent operate from a single priority in a given situation. An additional thirty-one percent use two priorities, and twenty-two percent operate from three. A very small proportion, approximately two percent, employs four or more simultaneously.

Most of us concentrate on one or two mindsets, which is reasonable. We set direction and focus energy on what we judge to be critical right now. However, this does not mean we should stop scanning for early signals that emerging issues may need immediate attention. We avoid knee-jerk decisions by using a systematic approach. A systematic approach will pay dividends with fewer surprises and more manageable risks. Considering the entire spectrum of mindsets enables us to hone in on the critical and recognize that all decisions must be elastic. Decisions cannot last forever in a turbulent marketplace.

Operating with one or two priorities at a time produces greater success than trying to cover every aspect all the time. Trying to do everything usually results in confusion, people working at cross purposes, and rework. In fact, a single priority boosts goal clarity and aligns efforts. But this focus does not mean we have circled the wagons and closed our minds. We must keep monitoring across all mindsets to detect change, reassess impact, and monitor ramifications.

Just a quick reminder: one priority is not "better" than another, any more than one color in a spectrum is better than another. Each has a special value. The key is to match the priority to the current business situation based on a careful examination of all factors.

Mastery of the big picture through mindset questions enables leaders to carefully calibrate their priorities to current circumstances. It is costly to zero-in on a plan that ends up missing the key target.

WHY PRIORITIES MUST SHIFT

As discussed in Chapter 1, most executives tend to make their decisions without considering alternatives. This might be due to ingrained habits, a desire to be seen as consistent, or an aversion to change. But failing to continually consider an existing decision from multiple points of view can result in missed opportunities. In the past, several firms—including IBM—declined to purchase the patent for xerography when a cost analysis suggested that no one would pay money for a machine that merely replaced inexpensive carbon paper. The logic was flawless from a cost-benefit viewpoint, but it was also much too narrow and, therefore, a missed opportunity.

Ignoring alternative mindsets can be dangerous. If an executive team decides to solely focus on the Performing Mindset (which prioritizes improving efficiencies) when it is trying to recruit and retain top talent, then it may experience a number of negative outcomes, such as disappointing recruitment efforts and high turnover. Trying to reestablish a reputation as an employer of choice following a poorly handled layoff, for example, is a daunting challenge.

Sticking with one mindset without checking if current circumstances have changed can also prove harmful. We live in a turbulent world; we must constantly monitor our environment and be willing to adjust to it.

Hockey great Wayne Gretzky famously stated that he skated to where the puck would be in the future rather than where it was at the moment. Mindset priorities, like pucks, should move. Let us assume, for example, that an organization has a problem with product quality. Its leaders may naturally prioritize a Performing Mindset. This makes sense, but once the quality problem is sufficiently addressed, the leaders may well need to prioritize a different mindset. Just as hunger is satisfied after a meal, once a priority has been addressed, another will likely dominate our attention.

THE DYNAMIC LEADERSHIP SPECTRUM WHEEL

The mindsets are connected, as illustrated in the Leadership Spectrum Wheel (see Figure Two). The sequence depicts the traditional progression of mindset priorities, which will be discussed in the following six chapters.

Figure Two. The Leadership Spectrum Wheel

The Leadership Spectrum Wheel also illustrates the organization life cycle. Though many of us assume that the organization life cycles end in death, organizations can drastically outlast the human life span. Time doesn't kill them—blunders do. Organizations can be renewed with brilliant leadership.

Details on how to use the wheel in team development, conflict management, and influence will be covered in later chapters.

Avoiding Blind Spots

When leaders fixate on one mindset, they wear blinders, ignoring things that might distract them. Although this can intensify focus, blinders also create dangerous blind spots that prevent a vision of the big picture and its risks. In fact, blinders are used in horse racing to remove distractions that might cause a horse to deviate from the racetrack. While using blinders is often advantageous in horse racing, it puts leaders at a disadvantage when they focus too narrowly. The trouble is that a racetrack is set, but competition, technology, and the economy are fluid. A wide and watchful view is essential in monitoring all the variables, permitting greater agility.

To prevent getting stuck with a single viewpoint, we must encourage diversity of thought and be open to new perspectives. We know the danger of having only "yes men" around us, so we need to foster a climate where all ideas are explored and where people feel that they can speak the truth to those in power. As journalist Walter Lippmann said, "When all think alike, no one thinks very much."

One way to create an open environment where viewpoints are explored is to use a checklist to sharpen thinking and document the scrutiny of alternatives. Just as checklists are used by doctors, pilots, and lawyers to ensure that issues are not overlooked, a "mindset checklist" ensures that multiple mindsets are identified and evaluated.

Choosing Mindsets' Unique Advantages

Mindsets cannot be equated with personal or leadership style, because mindsets change with new data and events. Your leadership approach remains relatively stable, unlike situations and circumstances, which are perpetually in flux. Change is a constant in every organization, and mindset priorities must be adjusted to meet new realities.

Golf balls, tennis trophies, family pictures, and other souvenirs adorn offices and give clues about a person's motivation or interaction **preferences, but** these do *not* reflect his or her mindset. Learning about people's hobbies, family, or past positions neither reveals the direction in which they want to head nor dictates what they will decide, approve, implement, or support. Their motivation reflects an aspect of their style, but it cannot inform you of their goals or actions.

Think about how you choose what to wear each morning. Your closet is full of options, but your selection will depend on the weather, the people you will encounter, or your schedule that day. The jacket you pick one day might be casual or formal depending on your day's activities, but it has nothing to do with your motivation or values. If you are moving boxes in offices, you would select something different than if you were making a presentation to key decision makers. The choice is situation-dependent—just as mindsets are —and does not reflect your values, personality, or motivation.

Understanding mindsets and selecting the most relevant priorities leads to success. It does not require a specific personality. After all, stellar CEOs display a wide array of characteristics and styles. Developing mindset effectiveness is also a great deal easier than trying to alter personal style or temperament.

Moving Out of Mental Ruts

By tapping into all six mindsets, we see things in a new light and can work to avoid mental ruts.

Let's take the example of an executive who was asked to head a product development project that would reposition his firm in its industry. He started by adopting an Inventing Mindset priority, with its emphasis on creating new products and services through synergies or discovery. He protected his innovation-oriented team from existing rules and procedures by creating a cocoon around them. The team's success gained organization-wide attention, and new resources were allocated to continue to accelerate their efforts.

The original tight-knit team expanded to meet the new demand, but new hires suffered when the only direction they received was to "get to work" with one of the existing teams. Without clear structure, responsibilities, and roles, productivity slipped. Clearly, role clarity and expectations were needed.

The leader was reluctant to impose such new requirements, fearing that this change would jeopardize innovation, energy, or enthusiasm. He equated more project structure to an overly controlled, hierarchy-bound dinosaur. Therefore, roles remained vague to avoid a "not my job" syndrome or reduced cooperation. Subsequently, confusion became widespread and problematic.

Once the executive understood and valued multiple mindsets, he was able to see beyond his entrenched and overly optimistic view that only a small, unencumbered and nimble team could succeed. He started monitoring and calibrating, and he found that creating new parameters could be adopted without sacrificing innovation. In fact, he discovered that an effective structure freed energies for creative pursuits. People could focus on getting work done rather than on navigating murky practices caused by weak systems, role confusion, and poor coordination.

Knowing When to Hold and When to Fold

Leaders are often described as dedicated, committed, determined, persistent, and consistent. Although each of these qualities has value, the larger stereotype encourages many leaders to "stick to their guns" or "stick to their knitting." When taken too far, this instinct results in what the great American poet Ralph Waldo Emerson referred to as "foolish consistency" that is the "hobgoblin of little minds." It encourages some to hold on to an announced course long past its expiration date.

Such intransigence may account for the dramatically increased CEO turnover rates of recent years. When a leader pursues one goal at all costs, the price to the organization and for the leader is very high.

A case study that describes the leadership of a mid-sized firm illustrates the need for adaptability and continued vigilance. Two engineers founded a U.S. telecommunications company to build modems and encryption devices. One of them served as president and grew the company to 3,000 employees based on a dedication to providing leading-edge products. As the business expanded, customer problems grew as a result of inadequate technical support and missed schedules. But the president kept his concentration on research and development, until major contracts were threatened.

The board replaced the president with the existing vice-president of sales, who was deeply committed to meeting customer needs. In short order, customer problems were resolved. But as business poured in, new problems surfaced in manufacturing. The second president delayed delving into operational details and was encouraged to retire.

A third president was committed to providing structure and revamping systems. Soon, things were running smoothly and the firm's reputation revived. At that juncture, an international firm purchased the company and installed the fourth president. Cost-cutting ensued in an effort to beef up financial returns. Unfortunately, the fourth (and last) president's decisions were insensitive to aspects of U.S. culture, and key engineering talent left, affecting both productivity and quality. At this juncture, it should not be surprising to read that the firm went bankrupt, leaving some perplexed at how a promising venture had soured in a matter of just a few years.

This failure can be attributed to leaders' unwillingness to consider the wider context, an overly consistent reliance on their original mindset, and an inattention to the turbulence confronting their technology-based firm. Each leader found success with one mindset and was unwilling to see the need for new ones.

So, while persistence and consistency are commendable, leaders must also be flexible. This is one of the many paradoxes leaders must navigate. Threading this needle requires balance, judgment, and an open mind combined with a willingness to listen to new ideas and stay alert to new realities. Viewing the world from the six mindsets encourages agility and wiser actions.

Avoiding "Groupthink"

Since teams are made up of multiple individuals, they tend to incorporate various opinions and priorities. But teams can also fall into the trap termed "groupthink." This happens when a group quickly adopts a single point of view because there is 1) an assumption that the decision has already been made, so the goal is to "go along to get along"; 2) a fear of rejection by the group if a new idea is expressed that diverges from past practice; 3) a feeling that loyalty requires fast acceptance; or 4) an illusion of invulnerability that leads individuals to believe that, no matter what decision is made, it will be solid. Whatever the cause, groupthink discourages creativity, individual responsibility, and effective decision making.

In his book *Victims of Groupthink*, famed research psychologist Irving L. Janis explored the critical nature of the group on thinking and decision making. As a means of examining the dynamic, he studied the decision-making processes of four U.S. presidents.

He found, for example, that President Kennedy's decision-making process failed in the Bay of Pigs invasion in Cuba. However, his handling of the Cuban missile crisis was internationally recognized as a success. The difference had nothing to do with his personality or intellectual prowess; it centered on his willingness to listen to people with different mindsets, his creation of small groups to develop new solutions, and withholding his thoughts until everyone had expressed their viewpoints.

When leaders recognize their impact on groupthink, they will see that their role is not to provide answers but to ask questions and encourage discussion. Using the mindset paradigm, leaders have a set of questions to elicit new perspectives and creative solutions.

Winning Them Over Using A Mindset Paradigm

Leaders can be true leaders only when others are willing to follow. Others are more likely to follow and offer their active support when leaders demonstrate that they want all points of view. Recognizing the diversity of priorities in a group boosts communication effectiveness. In fact, the "Platinum Rule" recommends giving others what *they* want instead of assuming that everyone concurs with your wants. The "Golden Rule" —that is, treat others as you would like them to treat you—does not always win support of followers to the same degree. We must learn to listen to what is driving others to obtain a true win-win.

Jude Olson, former manager of Organization Development and Leadership at Lockheed Martin Aeronautics, demonstrated her Catalyzing Mindset when she introduced Take Your Child to Work Day at the Fort Worth, Texas, facility, which manufactures fighter jets. Even though the concept was a "sure winner" with employees, there were other points of view that had to be considered. To make the project happen, Olson met with key stakeholders and listened to their views. The Vice President of Operations identified concerns relating to safety, liability, and work disruption. Accepting this point of view, Olson began working with the security, facilities, human resources, and operations staffs to reduce the perceived risk and allay fears of lost production. In addition, she created employee teams to plan logistics and services for the event. The teams not only resolved problems, but also created a buzz that became contagious.

Olson's infectious "can-do" attitude and her willingness to creatively search for win-win alternatives spread to the teams. One team developed a "tour lane" to direct the flow of visitors away from partially assembled jet engines as well as restricted areas. A Saturday was selected to ensure work was not disrupted and to enable school-aged kids to participate. They also decided that every child would be escorted by authorized employees, cameras would be banned, and a medical tent would be in place. Union cooperation was obtained, and a large number of volunteers signed up to help direct parking, traffic, signage, and security. Ultimately, the plan was approved, in part due to the thorough planning, which addressed major concerns and fears.

When the big day came, the anticipated four to five thousand attendees swelled to ten thousand. The event took place without a safety, security, or health-related incident. The high level of planning was evident; for example, four diaper-changing stations offered free diapers, wipes, and privacy. The president received numerous notes of appreciation, along with requests to expand the scope to grandchildren, nephews, and nieces. As a result, an annual "Family Day" was adopted not only at the Fort Worth facility but at other sites.

Olson considered all points of view, accepted others' perspectives, and found creative solutions. Her willingness to value each mindset led to the type of buy-in and support that formal requests or directives cannot match.

Finding Win-Win Solutions

Recognizing and valuing different mindsets reveals opportunities for mutually satisfying benefits. Seeing a situation from others' points of view enables you to meet their needs while also satisfying your own.

The story of a situation at a hospital chain illustrates how listening to the prevailing mindsets pays dividends. Hospital leaders identified a problem, which they labeled an ineffective physician-to-patient or staffing ratio, and they dispatched a consultant to one of their hospitals to fix this issue. Not surprisingly, when the consultant arrived from headquarters, her reception was chilly and defiant.

This situation could have degenerated into a conflict between "headquarters" and the "field," but the consultant averted the stand-off by listening to the medical staff. She found that the doctors were not concerned with the staffing ratios. Instead, they were bothered by the length of time patients had to wait for emergency appointments.

Rather than insisting on immediately pursuing her directive of studying staffing ratios, the consultant elected to analyze the doctors' primary concern: wait time. She confirmed that there was an inordinate delay in obtaining emergency appointments. With further investigation, she discovered that patients who requested an annual physical got earlier appointments than those who asked for emergency appointments. Of course, this resulted in many emergency patients switching their requests to a total checkup. Because annual health assessment appointments are longer, this practice reduced the number of patients seen each day by the physicians.

Once this information surfaced, the hospital implemented a new appointment process. Response time improved dramatically, as did physician-to-patient ratios. Meeting the field staff's mindset focus on customer satisfaction (i.e., Catalyzing Mindset) in turn produced the desired improvement in staffing ratios (i.e., Performing Mindset) sought by headquarters—a win-win.

SHARPENING YOUR MINDSET MASTERY

We must shift our mindsets when disconfirming information surfaces or when a situation dramatically changes. However, we must grasp the full picture before we jump to conclusions. This isn't rocket science but, rather, a step-by-step approach that values questioning over providing immediate answers and soliciting input over solo decision-making. When we address complex issues, uncertainty, or new opportunities, the steps are:

1. Start with a thoughtful identification of the issue. This requires considering all six mindsets to ensure that the issue is defined broadly enough to include both causes and symptoms.
2. Collect information to capture the whole picture. This can be verified using the mindset questions, which will be detailed in Chapter 10.
3. Identify how success will be measured by identifying the key metrics from each mindset.
4. Explore or brainstorm alternative solutions by asking mindset questions to stimulate creative thinking.
5. Evaluate the possible choices and select the most promising.
6. Examine the ramifications of the plan by looking at risks from each mindset lens.
7. Consult with key stakeholders to validate the assumptions and plans.
8. Implement and communicate using mindsets to address audience priorities.
9. Monitor and measure outcomes and make adjustments as needed.

The mindset framework produces the benefits of analysis and slow thinking. Comprehensive, creative, practical, and implementable steps require more time to collect and evaluate data, to confer with others, and to deal with potential conflicts. When faced with complex challenges, this framework is more likely to result in success and getting it right the first time.

Enhancing Agility During Turbulence

The prevalence of turbulence is clear, whether it's the dot-com mania, the Great Recession, new technology, changes in global competition, tsunamis or other natural disasters. We may yearn for past stability and predictability, when we felt we had a clear grasp of what we were facing and could "control" events. But wishing for simpler times does not alter the fact that today major forces are beyond our control. Our environment controls our lives more than ever and we must admit that our actions are driven by circumstances. Change is prevalent, unrelenting, and powerful.

The ability to cope with such change is not a matter of IQ, but mental agility. This dexterity is enhanced through a multi-mindset perspective that allows leaders to more effectively judge the internal and external environment. As circumstances change, mindsets and plans must change. We must make smarter decisions and adjust through mid-course corrections to survive and thrive in turbulent seas.

Leveraging the Organization Life Cycles

As we have already seen, mindsets stem from specific conditions, environmental realities, and complex systems. In addition to market or competitive realities, there are internal realities that influence decisions and plans. A large portion of these internal realities are reflected in the organization's "life cycle," which typically begins in a start-up phase and then progresses through five other phases (see Table Two).

Unlike human life cycles, an organizational life cycle does not necessarily end in death. With great leadership, decisions, plans, and cultures, organizations can endure for hundreds of years.

Organizational life cycle stages provide a practical framework for leaders to assess internal realities and potential barriers. Table Two illustrates the association between organization life cycle stages and the six critical mindsets.

Table Two: Mindsets and the Organization Life Cycle

Organization life cycle stage	Issue	Mindset
Start-up or rebirth	Creating new products and services	Inventing
Growth or "hockey stick"	Gaining market share, satisfying customers, ensuring fast response	Catalyzing
Stature	Building systems, policy, controls, and infrastructure	Developing
Prime	Improving quality, processes, and ROI	Performing
Maturity	Developing and retaining people, and maintaining a high-performing culture	Protecting
Renewal	Seizing opportunities and testing assumptions	Challenging

The organization typically launches with a start-up phase, when new products or unique services take precedence over issues such as policy formulation, process improvement, or employee development. Creating new offerings is the major focus. After pinpointing the product or service offering, the focus shifts to growing markets and satisfying customers. Increased market success brings new concerns and challenges. Leaders must now consider how to meet the demand, which means establishing new systems, adopting new policies to guide action, and creating an internal structure to support the growing operation.

After new structures are in place, the focus swings to how to make the operation more efficient with process improvement, cycle time reductions, and a boost in financial returns. Once operations are polished, the leaders seek to protect their accomplishment, and a new "maturity" phase begins, in which talent retention and sustaining the culture comes into prominence. Maturity issues also include succession planning, updating competencies, and sustaining internal brand or traditions. Some firms get stuck here, as if they have reached the perfect state and want to hold on firmly to current practices. This is a mistake. Equilibriums are not sustainable given the prevalence of wide-ranging change.

The final stage examines how to renew the organization by examining new business models, addressing new trends, identifying new niches, or shifting product lines. Renewal is the only way to avoid stagnation and failure. It requires a willingness to let go of outdated practices and seize new opportunities.

Each stage requires agile leadership, not static homage to past practices or cash-cow product lines. There is no guarantee that every organization will make it all the way around the life cycle. Stagnation can happen at any stage because of internal silos, poor succession planning, weak customer services, insufficient innovation, or new competition.

Focusing on one stage or one mindset is dangerous. As an example, consider the narrowly focused tech firms that existed prior to the dot-com bust, such as eToys. It was a promising Internet venture in 1997, but it underestimated the importance of structuring a fulfillment system. Its leaders tended to focus on start-up and growth, employing the Inventing and Catalyzing Mindsets, but paid insufficient attention to distribution issues. When some highly prized customers did not get their holiday orders on time, they spurned the site. Even after the company established new distribution centers, their reputation remained blemished. In 2009, the firm was acquired by Toys "R" Us.

Though the Organization Life Cycles in Table Two predicts a likely flow of stages, this sequence is not automatic or guaranteed. There are instances in which an organization must revert to a prior stage if circumstances warrant. New regulations, for example, may require new product or process innovation. Recessions may pull attention to cost-cutting, and new technology may require revisiting internal systems. A key person may face a major health challenge and resign, or an audit or whistleblower may reveal unknown problems. The U.S. Department of Veterans Affairs, for example, experienced a major shock requiring new priorities in 2014 due to whistleblowers exposing system failures.

Even if the progression deviates from the sequence in the Leadership Spectrum Wheel, the life cycle helps leaders detect which mindset is associated with each organization life cycle stage. Armed with this knowledge, leaders can more effectively cope with and address internal realities.

SUMMARY AND NEXT STEPS

The mindset framework serves a number of critical purposes, from managing conflicts to enhancing agility. It counters a leader's tendencies to think he or she already knows all that needs to be known. Some of the most difficult words for a leader to speak are "I do not know."

The mindset template ensures that more information is collected and applied to help you avoid blind spots that produce blunders. The mindset framework can be used at many decision-making stages, including when you are:

- Refining goals and plans based on new input.
- Providing a stimulus for brainstorming and idea generation.
- Preparing balanced criteria for evaluating ideas or alternatives.
- Considering the level of risk and potential ramifications of a particular decision.
- Providing key talking points to gain support for implementation.

The following six chapters delve into each mindset and provide lists of questions to help you achieve great decision-making and leadership. Cases and examples highlight effective applications as well as the dangers of overreliance on one mindset. As a result, you will gain a thorough understanding of each mindset and how it can be used to navigate uncertainty and complexity as well as enrich opportunities.

PART

TWO

Six
Results-Driven
Priorities

———

Valuing Creativity, Innovation and Synergies

The Inventing Mindset

To cease to think creatively is but little different
from ceasing to live.

—*Benjamin Franklin*

Creativity is part of human nature. It can only be untaught.

—*Ai Weiwei (designer of Beijing Bird Stadium)*

Imagination is more important than knowledge.

—*Albert Einstein*

"Creative people are not geniuses. They just think different," said Steve Jobs, the late and great CEO of Apple, Inc. This was certainly true in his case, whether he was running a film business (Pixar Animation Studios created the groundbreaking *Toy Story* movie series) or a consumer electronics business (blockbuster Apple products include the iPod, iPhone, and iPad).

But does every leader have to personally display such creativity to stimulate creative thinking? The answer is no. The Inventing Mindset—that is, a focus on the creation of new products and services that make others say, "Why didn't I think of that?"—stems from the cultural environment. And we need to create that environment in our fast-paced, interconnected world, since it is key to organizational survival. As Will Rogers said, "Even if you're on the right track, you will get run over if you just sit there." No one wants to run a company that manufactures eight-track tape recorders, telephone booths, or 3.5-inch floppy disks.

The Inventing Mindset prioritizes the creation of innovative products or services, of course, but it also emphasizes finding new uses for technology, determining innovative ways of working cross-functionally, adding enhancements to current products, and connecting existing products to new customers.

WHY LEADERS NEED THE INVENTING MINDSET

We may resist making innovation a top priority, especially if our organization's success is predicated on low-cost products (e.g., low-margin electronics, discount stores), slowly changing technologies (e.g., plumbing), or traditional offerings (e.g., certain types of restaurants). Indeed, skepticism is sometimes warranted: not all innovations succeed. Yet, nearly every organization must adapt to change, including religious organizations. The Pope now has both a Facebook and a Twitter account.

The Inventing Mindset can spawn grand ideas that lead to extremely successful businesses. FedEx Corporation is an example of a corporation that was originally based on innovation and outside-the-box thinking. FedEx—a leader in transportation, information, and logistics—was envisaged in an undergraduate economics term paper written by its founder Fred Smith at Yale University. Smith's term paper failed to impress his professor. After all, how could the shortest distance between two points always be through Memphis? However the concept has proven to be a winning one.

Dedicated to leading-edge thinking, FedEx grew rapidly by relying on invention. Some of its breakthroughs include the first bar-code labeling of packages, a handheld bar-code scanner system to track packages, and an onboard communications system that uses satellite tracking to pinpoint vehicle location. Such innovations have helped the organization live up to its promise— as summed up in a former ad campaign—to deliver when "it absolutely, positively has to be there."

FedEx launched SenseAware in 2000 to enable customers to continually monitor their shipment's location and temperature. Another innovation is its same-day delivery service. In 2004, FedEx expanded its service to seamlessly combine printing and shipping by purchasing the Kinko's chain.

FedEx relies on a creative, open corporate culture to continuously propel ideas and generate new opportunities. Each employee is expected to think creatively. It created a cross-discipline team, FedEx Innovation, with the charter to (1) identify emerging customer needs and technologies to change what is possible, (2) accelerate prototyping and shorten incubation time, and (3) ensure effective commercialization to stay on the leading-edge.

FedEx benefited from an Inventing Mindset, but there are many who suffered by failing to innovate or failing to take full advantage of breakthroughs. One of the most fabled, and paradoxical, examples of missed opportunities comes from the former Palo Alto Research Center (PARC), owned by Xerox. The center developed significant advances in computer science, which included, according to *High Tech History,* the "development of the laser printer, the Ethernet, a variation of ARPANET (a predecessor of the Internet); various e-mail delivery systems; the nucleus of the modern personal computer—featuring a monitor with graphical user interface, or GUI (pronounced 'gooey'); and the first modern version of the computer 'mouse.'"

Despite these amazing innovations, Xerox failed to capitalize on them, permitting Apple and Microsoft to introduce them. This illustrates that the Inventing Mindset is not just about having great ideas or superb research. After all we can all come up with new ideas, but transforming them into something that is useful is the essence of innovation. We also must work with others to harness support from the organization to develop and bring innovations to market.

FEATURES OF THE INVENTING MINDSET

The Inventing Mindset seeks stature as an industry leader, expands the product life cycle through product extensions, applies technology in novel ways, discovers new synergies within the organization, and explores the next "big thing." So, let's clarify the key thinking within the Inventing Mindset.

Don't Rest on Your Laurels

The Inventing Mindset remains a top priority when an organization assumes that the finish line in their industry is a moving target. This is particularly true in the fast-changing digital world. In fact, former Intel president Paul Otellini stated that Intel's goal is to make "obsolete" its current products by creating new products. This goal was consistent with Intel cofounder Gordon Moore's prediction that the number of transistors on a computer chip will double every eighteen months. "Moore's Law" has held true even longer than Moore himself anticipated.

Another former leader at Intel, Andrew ("Andy") Grove, is well known for his guiding motto, captured in his book title: *Only the Paranoid Survive*. It is this "never-take-anything-for-granted" type of thinking that has permeated Intel's culture. Yet, even with this strong culture and history of innovation, Intel was slow to shift their product line to meet the needs of smart phone providers.

Be Prepared

Creativity requires preparation and encouragement. Innovations seldom appear out of the blue. They stem from expertise, collaboration, experimentation, curiosity, and independence. The story of Edwin Land is a case in point. According to lore, one day he and his daughter were walking through the woods, admiring the fall foliage and taking pictures. Her question to him— "Why can't I see the pictures now?"—spurred Land to create the Polaroid camera. At first glance, the idea appears to be pure serendipity, but a more careful analysis reflects robust preparation.

As a youngster, Land slept with a copy of Robert Williams Wood's *Physical Optics* under his pillow because of his fondness for optics, light, electricity, and photography. Land attended Harvard University and, while in a freshman physics class, sought a way of producing an inexpensive polarizing lens. He was already an expert, not some overnight wonder who merely stumbled on a great idea in his spare time on a walk.

Preparation also marks the career of "the Wizard of Menlo Park," Thomas Edison. While the title implies magical powers, Edison was really a dedicated researcher with a strong collaborative team. Despite numerous patents on various inventions including the phonograph, mimeograph machine, stock ticker, telephone transmitter, and motion pictures, his success was not immediate. He is famously quoted as saying inventing is "one percent inspiration and ninety-nine percent perspiration."

After ten thousand experiments failed to produce a light bulb, some labeled the project a failure, but Edison disagreed. He retorted that he discovered ten thousand ways that would not work. It was not long thereafter that his persistence resulted in a solution.

Ask Questions

Thomas Edison's business fortunes also benefited from his willingness to ask questions. When General Marshall Lefferts, president of Gold and Stock Telegraph Company, offered to purchase Edison's multiple stock ticker patents, Edison asked him for a figure. When Edison heard the response of $40,000, he was surprised. It was substantially more than his expectation of $3,000 to $5,000.

The power of questions has only grown. In 2006, when Google CEO Eric Schmidt was interviewed by *Time* magazine, he stated:

> *We run the company by questions, not by answers. So in the strategy process we've so far formulated thirty questions that we have to answer.... You ask it as a question, rather than a pithy answer, and that stimulates conversation. Out of the conversation*

[47]

*comes innovation. Innovation is not something that I just wake up
one day and say 'I want to innovate.' I think you get a better
innovative culture if you ask it as a question.*

Google exemplifies a company that is not resting on its laurels or relying on past answers. What it really depends on is the right sets of questions. Smart questions produce great answers and solutions.

Try Something Different

At a time when large population centers were viewed as the best place to market, Wal-Mart founder Samuel Walton chose to focus on small towns. Flying under the radar of other retail organizations, the firm grew quickly until it dominated its industry and the Fortune 500 List, where it remains number one as of 2014.

Bucking conventional wisdom also paid dividends for Citibank. It was the first large financial institution to tap the college student credit card market. The stereotype of an unemployed student enjoying carefree days on campus missed the fact that many students have strong parental support and are working. Citibank realized that parents would welcome a student's access to a credit card for emergencies and that parents would likely cover the charges if a student failed to pay. Citibank created a new market niche and boosted its brand.

Rethinking old practices also led railroads to the concept of intermodal transportation, where containers are loaded on ships and easily transferred to land transport without having to rely on longshoremen to offload smaller crates, a practice that cost more and created delays.

Cirque du Soliel re-imagined the circus without the expense of animal acts. It also discarded the idea that the circus had to travel. Permanent shows in Las Vegas continue to draw huge audiences.

Another example of reimagining an industry has occurred in the wine business. It is now clear that there are more than two options in regard to wine production. Certainly there is a healthy prestige as well as a budget wine market. And, because not everyone wants to focus on the sommelier market, companies such as Yellow Tail have created mid-market wines that offer fun, ease of selection, and a sense of outback adventure. New packaging and branding opened another avenue. Wine packaged in a box rather than a bottle reduced shipping costs and also enlarged the market.

Trust Your Educated Insights

Sony cofounder Akito Morita recognized the potential of a portable music player (what eventually became the Walkman) without in-depth market research, saying, "The customer does not know what is possible; we do." He placed greater confidence in the Inventing Mindset than in customer feedback. Likewise, when Steve Jobs was asked about how much market research had gone into products such as the iPhone, he said, "None. It isn't the consumers' job to know what they want."

In 1988, then-Chrysler CEO Robert Lutz took a significant risk to establish Chrysler as a market leader. He proposed that the cash-strapped firm invest in a new two-seat sports car to change the public's low opinion of Chrysler's engineering skills. Despite weak financial analysis and concerns that the new vehicle would divert attention from Chrysler's ongoing revitalization efforts, Lutz persisted. The Viper not only changed people's view of Chrysler as an out-of-date car manufacturer but also spurred morale and helped retain key talent.

Cross-Fertilize

The Inventing Mindset can help uncover new opportunities across specialties and disciplines. In 1998, Celera Genomics was founded by Tom White and J. Craig Venter to sequence the human genome using both medical DNA research and the newer computer science field of bioinformatics.

In another example of productive partnerships, Siemens and Corning combined their expertise to form Seicor, which produced fiber optics. Corning offered deep experience in glass, silicone, and fiber optics, while Siemens, a German electronics giant, was a leader in telecom cable pursuing a larger U.S. market share. The 23-year-old partnership ended in 1999 when Corning purchased Siemens' share. Revenue had grown to $21 billion, and the experience established Corning as a leader in the telecom infrastructure sector.

The rising cost of developing and testing biotech products in the pharmaceutical industry triggered alliances and partnerships to ensure industry preeminence. Collaborating across medical specialties has led firms such as Eli Lilly to enter R&D cost sharing, licensing and distribution agreements, and joint ventures. Pharmaceutical companies and medical device manufacturers also partnered with universities to tap new skills.

Other successful combinations include Microsoft and Intel, Siemens and Disney, Starbucks and Barnes & Noble, and Starbucks and Pepsi (an alliance to create the Frappuccino). As a result of partnerships, what used to seem impossible is now feasible.

Create Processes that Invigorate

Inspiring innovative ideas and getting them to market is seldom simple. Ground-breaking concepts threaten routines, require new skill sets, compel investment, and disrupt products and practices. Therefore, fostering innovation requires deliberate support, encouragement, processes, and incentives.

Royal Dutch/Shell uses a process called GameChanger to accelerate grassroots technological innovation and turn concepts into reality. A team reviews internal proposals and decides, usually within one day, whether to fund them to the proof-of-concept stage. A second project review determines whether support will continue on into the development and commercialization process. GameChanger posts ideas for review by all employees to stimulate thinking, reduce risks, and identify potential synergies.

Innovation is not the sole province of private firms. Governmental agencies as well as nonprofit organizations benefit. A U.S. Department of Energy assistant secretary transformed his organization's suggestion process from a tedious paper exercise that merely reinforced the status quo into a more vibrant and streamlined system. Every quarter he held an "open house" that enabled employees to present new ideas and proposals. The caveat was that employees had to have fully analyzed and vetted the implementation hurdles and costs. In short order, this process produced new taxpayer services, an organizational realignment, and a streamlined workflow. These ideas had previously been withheld or stymied during the review process where few ideas were accepted. With the promise of a full investigation, the process was re-invigorated. A flurry of ideas were proposed and everyone understood why they were accepted, rejected, or put on hold pending more information.

Other strategies can work as well. SAIC, a research and engineering firm, holds a "meetings week" where top leaders and high potentials explore and exchange ideas across the organization's locations and divisions. These generate insights, proposals, and pilot programs.

Be Willing to Fail

Even "failures" can be transformed into success stories. Apple's "Lisa" computer paved the way for outstanding future products. In the same way, Apple's false start with the Newton paved the way for the iPhone and iPad. Apple learns from experience, while many other firms squelch learning by failing to examine unsuccessful launches or to use post mortems. Even when a review is held, it can be performed in a perfunctory manner. Sometimes, the exercise becomes a thinly veiled effort to find a scapegoat, sending the message that new ideas might be career-ending mistakes.

Innovation doesn't guarantee success, but the chance of blunders increases without the benefits that reflection provides. The 1957 Edsel, for example, had a grille that was compared to a mouth sucking on a lemon, but this reaction indicated that design—instead of merely horse power and chrome—was becoming a critical factor in the car-buying process. The 1975 gull-wing stainless steel DeLorean captured attention when most major auto firms were producing indistinguishable cars. Most manufacturers now recognize that design is critical not only in fashion but also in home products, equipment, furniture, offices, and, of course, autos.

Another failure that informed a subsequent product launch was RJ Reynolds' smokeless cigarettes. Today, e-cigarettes are the fastest-growing tobacco market segment. And Maxwell House's ready-to-drink coffee was the precursor to the single-serve coffee machine.

Not all missteps lead to successful second acts, of course. Being willing to fail should not be equated to shooting for the moon or "betting-the-ranch." Pepsi's Crystal soda, Colgate's Kitchen Entrees, Life Savers' soda, Microsoft's WebTV, and BenGay aspirin are products that might have benefited from more vetting, using multiple mindsets.

Consider Collaborations

The days of the "lone inventor" have largely passed. Even when the image of the sole inventor was popular, it was frequently wrong. Thomas Edison worked with a team. He listed their names on patents—just after his name. While Steve Jobs is given credit for Apple's inventions, his ideas were brought to life by talented teams.

Individuals cannot expect to operate undisturbed in a lab for long stretches or expect every project to be a home run. The potential for success increases with interaction with other people, stimulating ideas from other disciplines and support from champions who can facilitate authorization and funding. Some scholars even believe that today's technologies and specialties are simply too complex to be understood by one person. Kellogg School of Management professor Benjamin Jones, for example, has argued that inventors must specialize in narrow domains and deeply rely on other experts and teamwork to discover breakthroughs.

Collaborations exist not only internally but also as a result of external alliances. Three U.S. Department of Defense (DOD) engineers working on microwave radio transmission technology formed Parateck Microwave in 1998. As a result of their collaboration, they found a method for sending information over radio waves on any frequency using a single antenna, increasing the efficiency of wireless networks and enabling the same equipment to be used around the world. After starting the firm, the engineers quickly negotiated a licensing agreement with the DOD to apply their work to the private sector while continuing to serve the DOD. In other examples, Disney's alliance with HP produced the Mission: Space ride at Epcot theme park, and BP and Schlumberger pooled resources and talent to develop horizontal well drilling tools.

Other Features

In addition to providing the benefits discussed previously, deploying our Inventing Mindset enables us to potentially aid creativity and originality when we:

- Encourage others to imagine new possibilities
- Show that new ideas are welcomed
- Support intelligent risk-taking
- Require innovative solutions to difficult issues
- Provide resources and remove potential barriers to innovation
- Listen and synthesize ideas
- Use creative thinking and problem-solving techniques effectively
- Explore how to integrate ideas, products and systems

SELECTING THE INVENTING MINDSET AS A PRIORITY

Should you adopt an Inventing Mindset as your top priority? That depends on your circumstances and challenges. For instance, if your competition is introducing new products, if your key customers have new requirements, if new technology offers a leap forward, or if new organizational synergies surface, then the Inventing Mindset likely takes precedence.

Consider, for example, how many "big-box" retailers were slow to recognize the paradigm-changing nature of the Internet. Suddenly, book behemoth Barnes & Noble, electronic chain store Circuit City and the music industry suffered as Internet shopping and downloads "came out of nowhere" to alter consumer behavior.

The Inventing Mindset becomes a top priority for stagnating or mature companies whose growth has plateaued. Consider the case of the Minnesota Mining and Manufacturing Co., now known as 3M, which was founded in 1902 to mine a mineral deposit for grinding-wheel abrasives. The company pivoted and reinvented itself through the process of innovation as the original product line struggled. Today, we certainly don't associate 3M with grinding and sandpaper.

In fact, 3M invests heavily in research and development. Why? Because it produces results. Whereas in 2008, about a quarter of the company's revenue came from products created in the previous five years, these days that number is up to 34%.

Of course, innovation is not always the most pressing issue. At times, hiring and retaining the workforce, concerns over customer satisfaction, or worries over supply chain become critical. But most organizations will benefit by keeping a close eye on the Inventing Mindset. Weaving innovation into your thinking even when stressing another point of view enables you to quickly "shift gears" as circumstances change and opportunities emerge.

AVOIDING IMBALANCES

The Greek dictum of moderation in all things applies to mindsets as well as action. Overemphasis on the Inventing Mindset can become problematic. If we become too enamored with a potentially breakthrough proposal that promises new stature as an industry leader, our judgment can become clouded. The following indicators *might* signal imbalance.

1. Innovations consume an extraordinary amount of funding or attention.
2. Recommendations target an entirely new and untested customer base.
3. Plans are operationally unfeasible.
4. Proposals require a totally new distribution channel.
5. Recommendations are overly elegant or expensive for the intended customer.
6. Proposals pursue low-quality solutions.
7. Suggestions ignore significant implementation and production barriers.
8. Proposals overlook basic cost-benefit analysis.
9. Initiatives require new competencies and skill sets.
10. Current customer behavior is assumed to be easy to change.
11. Skipping the "proof of concept" phase

Not one of these is automatically a "deal breaker," but each should be considered a red flag for careful review. If several indicators surface, there is a high need for a broad and deep mindset reexamination.

We cannot wish creative solutions into reality, and we cannot be beguiled by the "next big thing." We must monitor our assumptions and actions. Do we shift too quickly from one initiative to start the search for the next? Are we so enamored with finding something new that we overlook learning from past actions? Do we take the time to institutionalize the change, or is osmosis expected to do the job? And, finally, are we alert to the need to modify or alter a plan after its rollout?

ASSESSING CURRENT CONDITIONS

The Inventing Mindset requires balance. Innovation can disrupt existing operations, render treasured offerings obsolete, disturb key customers, or cannibalize existing inventory or locations. But we can easily go to the other extreme and fall into the habit of holding onto the past, concentrating on the short-term, rejecting risk and uncertainty, and failing to consider productive alliances. So, how can you assess your organization's support for innovation?

First, we can assess the degree to which our actions reflect those associated with the Inventing Mindset, mentioned earlier in the Features of the Inventing Mindset section. Second, we can assess the broader climate, including organizational support, corporate culture, and recognition and rewards. Asking the following questions help with this assessment.

Organization Support Questions

- Is there a plan or process for encouraging innovation?
- How much time, access, or money is allocated to uncovering new products/services?
- Is there a clear goal that supports innovation?
- Are new ideas clearly solicited and evaluated promptly?
- Does the organization enable people to follow their areas of interest?

- Do metrics gauge the level of innovation, the number of new products/services launched, or the sales volume gained as a result of new products/services?
- Are there planned opportunities to share ideas and explore synergies?
- How frequently and formally are new ideas considered? How effectively are employees engaged in the evaluation process?
- Are proposals and suggestions fully evaluated with feedback given to the originator?
- Is the organization prepared to support internal or external collaborations to spur innovation?
- Are innovators offered the opportunity to develop their ideas? (For example, some companies allow employees to spend a certain proportion of their work week on innovative projects which interest them.)
- Does the company leverage cross-functional task forces, provide skunk works, conduct pilot programs, and/or hold internal conferences?
- Is training offered in creative, lateral, critical, or analytical thinking?

Culture-Related Questions

- Does fear stifle engagement?
- Are suggestions expected from everyone?
- Are brainstorming, groupware, and organizational meetings used to expand thinking?
- Does every idea have to offer a slam dunk success?
- Are creative minds haunted by the specter of becoming scapegoats?

Recognition and Reward Questions

- Who was the last person promoted? Is this person noted for creative thinking?
- Can creative people advance their careers without following a managerial career path?
- Are there rewards for new ideas, even those that don't end up as blazing success stories?

- What types of rewards are offered for new ideas, suggestions, or patents?
- What type of recognition is offered to those who share information or insights or effectively collaborate with others?

SHARPENING THE INVENTING MINDSET

If you decide to bolster the use of the Inventing Mindset, the following questions can jump-start this practice by inspiring creative thinking:

What will encourage "outside the box" thinking? Not only can this discussion identify incentives that spur creative thinking, it can uncover current impediments to creative thinking.

What alternatives or new approaches are there? Everyone has ideas about new approaches, processes, or practices, but most fail to voice those ideas. Just asking this question signals openness to new ideas.

What can be learned from other functions, disciplines, product lines, or organizations? Innovation often arises from the cross-fertilization and integration of ideas across disciplines, functions, or units, but this can only happen when there is effective communication across units as well as a keen interest in learning.

What new combinations or synergies are possible? New technologies and processes can simplify practice, streamline communication, reduce redundancies, and monitor progress. Asking this question stimulates thinking about new ways of doing things.

What new options should be identified before analysis and evaluation start? Too often, teams move directly from data collection into the solution analysis phase without considering a range of new options and untraditional alternatives.

[57]

aints, what could we do differently? Removing existing releases new ways to approach processes, policy, structure.

ıct or service? The question promotes thinking beyond customer base, competitive landscape, technology, skill sets, and resources. When we are free to envision new possibilities, dramatic improvements can follow.

What will take our existing procedures/methods to new levels? We are frequently trapped by our current success and fail to search for even better products or services. To spark innovative thinking, we need trust, engagement and ownership in the culture.

What technologies are not being fully utilized? Technologies change rapidly, and, though we are often aware of such changes in our fields, we remain hemmed in by our current use and rely on outdated tools.

What competencies are not being fully utilized? Many feel their abilities are underutilized and would welcome greater challenges, responsibility and participation.

What would we learn if we were working to achieve the opposite results? Considering the opposite goal can be funny, freeing and productive. It uncovers existing impediments, old assumptions, and new potentialities, and it demonstrates a willingness to challenge existing practices.

What has never been tried before? This question uncovers good alternatives as well as new ways of working together. Certainly it encourages thinking beyond traditionally safe replies.

What was rejected or has failed in the past that might be viable now? Innovation can be stymied by the "already tried that" response. But times change, and something that was attempted yesterday may be viable today.

SUMMARY AND NEXT STEPS

Whether we adopt the Inventing Mindset as our current priority, we need to appreciate and value the perspective. New technologies, changing customer preferences, new variations, and new competitors appear from unexpected places and open new windows of opportunity. Consider how quickly the Walkman, single-feature mobile phone, entry-level digital camera, and stand-alone GPS device have lost their standing in the market. Virtually all organizations must remain alert to the opportunity for innovation, especially when turbulence and complexity abound.

Take the example of Dell. At the time of this writing, Dell seems to be feeling the effects of a downward trend in people's interest in personal computers. *CNET* reports, "Worldwide PC shipments, including desktops and laptops, suffered their seventh consecutive quarter of decline last quarter. . . . Over the last two years, tablets and smartphones have replaced PCs—contributing to the decline." As a result, at the time of this writing, substantial layoffs are rumored to be in the works at Dell.

Yet, Dell was built on customization and market innovation. Founder Michael Dell updated the direct marketing strategy when he founded the computer company. It designed its products to customer specifications, manufactured the machines, and sold directly to the customer. The company was the first to sell computers on the Web, and for five years it achieved a remarkable 54% annual growth while increasing earnings by more than forty percent. Dropping out of college with $1,000 to seed his new venture, Michael Dell focused on offering customers affordable equipment with reliable service. Building to order enabled the company to avoid the burden of carrying product inventory, and working directly with the customers eliminated third-party markup. As a result, inventory costs were low. A Dell executive described the firm by stating: "You've never seen an organization like this before—the pace, the information flow, the urgency all the time."

In short, Dell began as a major market and product innovator but then switched its focus to a Performing Mindset (covered in Chapter 6), which involved targeting cycle time, efficiency, and financial return. So, why is Dell in trouble today? One theory is that it was slow to switch to the tablet market because its leaders paid too little attention to changing technology and customer preferences. It appears to have been caught off-guard in a fast-shifting industry. Only time will tell how quickly it rebounds.

The excitement and, sometimes, glamour of the Inventing Mindset is not necessarily an organization's secret sauce. Hatching promising ideas without adequate planning, sufficient resources, proper skill matches, or commitment wastes time and energy. We must not introduce new ideas just for the fun of it or for the mistaken notion that if we are first to market everything will be smooth sailing.

Even when the organization executes an innovation superbly, it won't be brilliant unless the innovation resonates with the customers as clearly superior to other available offerings. Innovation blunders can damage bottom lines and reputations. For examples, think about the outcome of New Coke, Microsoft's WebTV, Apple's Mac G4 Cube, or the supersonic Concord.

Such failures likely demonstrate how the quest for innovation can outstrip customer requirements or interests. Sometimes, it is more important to listen to the market, customers, and the competition. These are key concerns of the Catalyzing Mindset, and that is the subject for our next chapter.

Just Do It
The Catalyzing Mindset

The way to get started is to quit talking and start doing.

−Walt Disney

Ideas won't keep. Something has to be done with them.

−Alfred North Whitehead

The customer is always right.

−Unknown

The Catalyzing Mindset prizes fast action to gain and keep customers. From this point of view, the customer is king, queen, or star, depending on the demographic. This mindset optimistically assumes that dedicated effort can move mountains, surmount barriers, and ensure customer loyalty. Nike's trademark slogan, "Just Do It," reflects a focus on action, as does Star Trek's Captain Picard's direction to his staff on the bridge to "make it so." Driven by a strong desire to get things done, this mindset uses inspiration, influence, and practical problem resolution to produce results.

WHY LEADERS NEED THE CATALYZING MINDSET

In a fast-moving world, nearly all of us have been in a "just get it done" mindset at one time or another. The Catalyzing Mindset values speed and passion over flawless execution. It assumes that "time is of the essence" and that being first in the market is a competitive advantage. When we operate from this mindset, we want full responsibility for producing results. Therefore, we prefer to work with those who are highly committed, action-oriented, and willing to go above and beyond the call of duty.

This mindset's desire for quick responses is easy to recognize, even though results cannot be assured. Sometimes the desire for quick responses is effective, while at other times it is recklessly impetuous. That's because the "we can do it" mode often necessitates navigating around standard practices and policies. Negotiation and persuasion can smooth out some issues, but when they cannot, those operating from this mindset invoke Rear Admiral Grace Hopper's motto: "It is easier to ask for forgiveness later than get permission today." In other words, act first and calm troubled waters later.

The Catalyzing Mindset uncompromisingly concentrates on customers, competitors, and market position. When we select this mindset, we zero in on shifting competitive forces, customer requirements, technological advancements, and user experiences. To gauge success, this mindset's yardsticks include expanding market size and territory, increasing sales volume, thrashing the competition, and seizing hot new trends.

This mindset's action orientation stems from the conviction that everyone will rise to the challenge once they know what is expected and have the tools to get the job done. Initiative, speed, and persistence in achieving goals are expected. And, when someone demonstrates a desire to excel, they are given greater autonomy. Goal accomplishment is rewarded with increased engagement, recognition, and new challenges.

Just as a military leader clearly instructs a unit to "take that hill," those of us who are using the Catalyzing Mindset focus on setting clear goals and outcomes for others to achieve, with the expectation that these goals will be not only be met but exceeded. To stay on top of changing opportunities, others are expected to display agility and initiative. The "bottom line" is on results rather than on following formal procedures or providing well-crafted plans, which might hamper a rapid response to new opportunities.

Adopting this mindset means that we want others to do whatever is necessary to meet market and customer requirements. Individuals' energies must be unencumbered by red tape so that they can go above and beyond a job description or organizational boundaries.

The mindset's zealously optimistic and extremely confident orientation means that words such as "no," "cannot," and "won't" are unacceptable. Instead, responses are expected to be "no problem," "will get right on it," and "of course"—even when the task appears overwhelming. Since the Catalyzing Mindset is prone to bullish forecasts and confidence that what is possible is also probable, directions tend to avoid jargon, minute detail, or equivocation. Instead of shrinking from a challenge, this mindset is emboldened by it. If glitches or problems surface, the Catalyzing Mindset immediately seeks a solution or workaround to keep things on track and on schedule.

While some operating from this mindset appear extroverted, this mindset should not become associated with charisma or other personality traits. Individuals with this mindset want to win and excel regardless of whether they have quiet, introverted personalities or outgoing, effusive personalities. The range of personalities focused on winning can be seen in the different personalities of football coaches. Tony Dungy, who led the Indianapolis Colts to a Super Bowl win and authored *Quiet Strength,* operates very differently than Pete Carroll, the coach of the 2014 Super Bowl winners, the Seattle Seahawks. While Dungy is very reserved, Carroll is noted for being a highly demonstrative, cheerleader type of coach, but both focus on action, resilience, and winning.

FEATURES OF THE CATALYZING MINDSET

The Catalyzing Mindset is paramount when it is time to introduce a new product, when new customers have been identified, when customer expectations shift, or when new competitors or products emerge. In other words, there will always be opportunities to adopt this perspective, so let's clarify how some leaders and organizations have successfully leveraged this mindset.

Demonstrate a Passion for the Customer

Mary Kay Ash's career demonstrates how targeting each customer segment both locally and globally pays dividends. As Ash's Horatio Alger-type biography illustrates, she combined sharp customer understanding with a swift response to capture opportunities. She tapped an overlooked stay-at-home workforce and gave them the chance to become entrepreneurs with almost unlimited freedom combined with financial benefits. With her life savings of $5,000, Ash launched Mary Kay cosmetics in 1963. She had early success, but she did not let this divert her from staying close to her customers. She reformulated products for specific markets. Customization, personal contact, and service enabled thousands of independent beauty consultants to vie for a pink Cadillac, which was awarded for outstanding sales. This fleet also served as an effective advertisement strategy.

Ash delivered dynamic and motivational speeches with the admonishment, "When you come to a roadblock, take a detour." Her "can-do" attitude imbued the organization with a clear priority of paying attention to the customer and persistent effort. As a result, Mary Kay grew from a small direct-sales company to the fifteenth-largest direct seller of skin care products in the world.

Of course, there are many ways of focusing on customers. Following are examples from other well-known firms:

- Personalized service at Nordstrom
- Fast service from ServiceMaster and Amazon Prime
- Extensive selection at Home Depot and Best Buy
- Low-price promise at Wal-Mart
- Easy-access facilities close to home at Wells Fargo and McDonald's
- Status prestige at Tiffany and Gucci

Customers are an organization's lifeline to a promising future. And to keep customers loyal, we have to deliver value and ensure that they feel appreciated. This commitment has to be more than lip service or a placard on the wall. It requires close monitoring. Factors driving the customer's buying decision change quickly. We need look only at the fashion industry or digital products to understand how tastes and preferences change. What is considered "cool" is driven by customers, the media, and social networks. Keeping up with customer preferences, market realities, and technology remains a perpetual necessity. Getting it right at the beginning is just a start; you have to keep delivering what is right at the start by evaluating all points of view.

Serve Internal Customers as Well

Not every person who prioritizes the Catalyzing Mindsets concentrates on external customers. Professional units within a firm have internal customers, typically legal, human resources, accounting, compliance, and quality departments. For example, consider procurement operations. In many firms, it is considered a major speed bump that slows action. However, in other organizations, procurement staff members work closely with project managers as they prepare purchase orders, draft contract specifications, or consider lease agreements. A customer-oriented procurement function operates very differently than one that is merely focused on compliance. With a customer service goal, attention is given to building bridges to internal customers and partnering with them to expedite services.

Internal customer service can also be provided by multidisciplinary or cross-functional teams. Lockheed Martin Corporation created a cadre of subject matter experts (SMEs) to serve internal "clients." Working to improve quality and competitiveness, the SMEs worked across business lines, disciplines, and organizational units to remove barriers to outstanding performance.

Quickly Seize Windows of Opportunity

The Catalyzing Mindset seeks to capture new opportunities before they evaporate or are harvested by others. In 2004, Mark Zuckerberg created a social networking site for Harvard students; its popularity quickly spread to other colleges, eventually revealing opportunities beyond the college campus. His next foray focused on high school students. Zuckerberg then recognized a larger market and quickly expanded beyond educational settings. In 2014, Facebook's registered users grew to 1.28 billion, and the company's value ballooned. By moving quickly, Zuckerberg solidified Facebook's position in social media and created a dominant position, discouraging other competitors from entering the networking marketplace.

Facebook created a new industry, but windows of opportunities also exist in established markets, if a new application for the product can be established. Consider the forty-year-old radio frequency identification chip (RFID), whose application focused on inventory control at a single location. The MIT Auto-ID Center discovered new applications for the chip in shipping, transportation, and retail. They spun their technology off to EPCglobal. Today, Walmart, Tesco, and the U.S. government require their suppliers to use RFID technology.

Not all windows of opportunity are in information technology. For example, Procter & Gamble introduced Pampers, the first disposable diaper, preempting other firms. Entering a market early, even if it starts out as a niche market, offers advantages that the Catalyzing Mindset seeks.

React Quickly to Customer Concerns

Those operating from Catalyzing Mindsets set clear goals to enable front line employees to rapidly rectify customer concerns and inspire action. Front-desk clerks at the Ritz-Carlton, for example, are authorized to generously adjust a guest's bill if there is a dispute— without having to check with a manager.

Nordstrom's legendary customer service was put to the test when a customer asked for a credit for a product that was never sold by the firm—ski boots. The customer got it.

But customer satisfaction encompasses more than personal interactions and problem resolution. When Johnson & Johnson's brand and reputation was threatened in the 1982 Tylenol® tampering case, the entire product line was recalled. The company made the decision, not mandated by the government, to demonstrate their commitment to quality, safety, and satisfaction. That action increased their brand's stature, sustaining its market position.

Various other companies have also found themselves confronting major customer distress. Ralston Purina voluntarily reported a potential problem in cattle feed and recalled the product in light of the public's concerns about mad cow disease. In 2013, Target® responded to a major security breach by offering credit monitoring for customers, rapidly replacing debit cards, and re-examining options for increased security at the point of sale. Even so, Target sales stumbled. It is interesting to learn that, ten years earlier, Target had considered the use of microchips on credit and debit cards but dropped the idea due to installation costs and potential processing industry resistance. That decision will likely be revisited. Recently Sam's Club announced it will start using chips on their membership cards and others are quickly adopting the idea for added security.

In contrast, firms that ignore defects, real or potential, dance to a dangerous tune. Ford and Firestone initially dragged their feet on recalling tires on SUVs until increasing customer and government complaints rang alarm bells so loudly they grabbed media attention. Likewise, Toyota was slow to address concerns with accelerator pedal problems despite a National Highway Traffic Safety Administration (NHTSA) notice and customer concerns. The firm, which had been the number-one selling car brand in the U.S., suffered some severe bashing in the media. Later, the firm announced that the issue was caused by floor mats interfering with the gas pedal. Other recalls that followed were the result of problems with air bag deployment, drive shafts, electric power steering, and crankshafts. Toyota's focus on growth had come at the cost of quality.

Most recently, General Motors suffered from revelations that it ignored ignition switch problems for years and that deaths resulted from the issue. NHTSA leveled a $3.5 billion fine in 2014 for late notification of the problems. After reviewing other issues, GM announced further recalls covering 13.8 million vehicles. Their new CEO, Mary Barra, insisted on complete reexamination of any potential problem and promised to promptly remedy the quality problems. Her lack of stonewalling deviated from past practice and enabled GM to largely maintain its market share.

Set Audacious Goals

Whether serving internal or external customers, the Catalyzing Mindset boldly challenges current practices, defines success in customer terms, inspires initiative, encourages significant change, and spurs action. Sometimes the term "big hairy audacious goal" (BHAG) summarizes the type of objective that is used to inspire and unite a company operating with this mindset. Whatever the term, we use this mindset to guard against complacency, mediocrity, extreme caution, and burdensome constraints encourage a strong customer focus.

For Honda, the BHAG was entering the U.S. motorcycle market in 1962 and competing against the entrenched and adored player, Harley-Davidson. Honda's first foray was less than spectacular. They tried to go head-to-head with Harley with large cycles that lacked the appealing Harley "rumble." However, Honda learned something by looking at their own staff, many of whom rode scooters that attracted considerable interest from bystanders. A new market was found centering on a smaller cycle that was seen as being more fun. Their tagline became, "You meet the nicest people on a Honda"—an effective indirect reference to the stereotype that gang members and "undesirables" rode Harleys. After winning kudos for their smaller machines, Honda successfully moved up-market to larger engines.

Capitalize on Customer Loyalty

Honda dented Harley-Davidson's market share. Vowing to fight back, Harley's Vaughn Beals and Richard Teerlink restored the brand to health by capitalizing on fierce customer loyalty. The formation of the Harley Owners Group (H.O.G.) drew riders into parking lots to rekindle their love of their Harleys and added new luster to the brand. The strategy also worked to soften the image of Harley owners, since the friendly group gatherings countered the stereotypical gang image. There was another benefit: it permitted Harley's market researchers to gain an in-depth knowledge of their customers' needs and wants. This strategy restored market growth to the point that Harley needed a waiting list for buyers. Most firms would love to have that kind of customer problem.

Expanding market scope through customer loyalty and brand reputation was also adopted by Mercedes-Benz. Having already captured a substantial portion of the luxury market, Mercedes elected to grow by offering less expensive cars to younger buyers. Balancing the prestige of their S-class with the relative affordability of the new entry-level C-class was carefully calibrated and studiously examined. This approach differed from that of the Japanese auto industry, which separates their luxury brands from their existing mass market product line.

Retaining customer loyalty requires flexibility. The cost of poor or inadequate service can lose current customers. Since retaining customers has many advantages, including economic ones, many firms work to keep key customers. Financial institutions waive late fees for customers in "good standing." In addition, loyalty programs offer special benefits to key customers. Some extremely special customers have elite status accompanied by special perks on everything from shopping to cruise ships.

Customers are the reason the organization exists because they assure a profitable future. Every organization attests that customers are key, and the Catalyzing Mindset guarantees that they are center stage when goals and decisions are being determined.

Avoid Over-Promising and Under-Delivering

Because the Catalyzing Mindset is interested in market growth, there is the potential that expansion may overwhelm the organization's capacity to meet the increased demand. Being able to service growing customer demand is critical to customer retention and brand reputation. Often, customers will be disappointed by the organization's inability to handle on-time deliveries, poor customer service, product outages, or inadequate ecommerce. Dissatisfied customers are costly because they tend to inform others of their poor treatment.

Toys "R" Us encountered problems in the late 1990s, showing that even established businesses aren't immune to scaling problems. Charles Lazarus dedicated his store to young children in 1948, just in time for the baby boomer generation. He grew the business by responding when his customers requested furniture and toys for older children. Eventually, he had a full-scale, market-dominating chain with more than 1,500 stores—a clear category killer. His catalog, stores, and prices set a benchmark in the toy industry.

In 1998, Toys "R" Us formed toysrus.com for continued growth. During the 1999 holiday season, however, the site was overwhelmed with online customer orders, which they were unable to be fulfill due to server failures and low inventory. The decision to notify customers that their orders had been canceled turned Toys "R" Us into the Grinch that crushed a holiday spirit. A storm of protest and outrage followed. Hot Christmas holiday toys must appear as promised in order to retain customers and a maintain a solid reputation.

Another holiday letdown occurred in 2013 when UPS was unable to deliver all its packages before Christmas. This was the result of a disconnect between what online merchants promised and what UPS could deliver. Understandably, online merchants hoped to bring in last-minute shoppers who were promised on-time delivery. However, the barrage of late orders overwhelmed UPS plans and staffing. Infuriated customers complained that they could not "trust" online shopping. UPS promised to rectify the matter with improved forecasting, better coordination with online retailers, and additional seasonal staffing.

Stay Alert to Potential Distortions

Distortions do not just happen during holidays. Sometimes customer feedback is misrepresented or warped. A governmental agency striving to improve customer service discovered that one of their field offices reported an exceptionally strong level of customer service. As you would expect, a team was sent to investigate and report on how this location achieved such stellar results. Instead of uncovering strong performance that could be shared across the agency, the team found a twisted feedback process. Taxpayers were asked to complete their customer satisfaction survey *before* getting service. To make the problem even worse, the client was expected to give their "feedback" to the person from whom they would receive service before they were actually served. Needless to say, the evaluations were high, reflecting the customer's hope of getting service. After all, it would be brazen to complain in advance to the person who could provide the desired service. Despite hours of waiting for service and frequently being sent from one person to another, customers reported being extremely satisfied with the service they had yet to receive. In reality, the feedback system had been cleverly manipulated.

Distortion exists in the private sector, too. Car dealers, for example, may offer customers free oil changes if they respond favorably to national surveys. Therefore, the prominently displayed plaques or the awards in dealer showrooms may not actually depict excellence.

Online reviews can also be skewed. A business may enter false reviews of a competitor to drive business away from that competitor. Sometimes owners encourage positive reviews with discounts and, at times, provide their own reviews. A five-star rating might mislead—or it might be accurate. A potential customer must consider who gave the rating and for what reason.

Listen Carefully

Sometimes we fail to actually listen or appreciate our customers because we believe we already understand all we need to know or that we know more than they do. In some cases, this might work (e.g., Steve Jobs at Apple), but most of the time this assumption places a company on the threshold of tragedy.

A business consultant's recent experience illustrates the benefit of careful customer attention. He was the third consultant hired to conduct an organizational study. Recognizing that his predecessors were talented professionals, he planned to decline the project. Then he decided to listen more carefully to his potential client. After asking the CEO what he wanted, he heard a response he would never have expected. The CEO explained that he wanted a report organized in eight sections with specified headings and in a blue binder. Aware that letting the client select the color of the cover, the number of dividers, and some generic headings didn't impinge on his freedom or ethics, the consultant accepted the engagement. He conducted his own analysis and delivered his report organized under eight tabs in a blue cover. The CEO not only praised the report but also implemented the recommendations. Even listening to "silly" customer requests can prove productive.

Customer requirements for new packaging size, faster delivery, better return policies, and more reliability cannot be ignored for long. Customers' behavior shifts drastically when they feel ignored or their preferences are overlooked. JC Penney's 2013 decision to offer lower prices as a replacement for holding "sales" was based on the assumption that shoppers hated clipping coupons. The assumption was only partially correct, and it cost sales—and the CEO's dismissal. Trying to change customer behavior based on a theory instead of on extensive customer awareness proved hazardous.

Netflix also lost touch with subscribers in 2011 when it announced a new policy requiring that customers have two accounts: one for DVD mail delivery and another for streaming. They lost 800,000 customers in the third quarter and suffered a stock dip of twenty-five percent. Their concerns about long-term projections for streaming media had overshadowed their focus on the customer until the uproar revised their thinking and pricing model.

Other Features

In addition to the features noted above, the Catalyzing Mindset tends to do the following:

- Build excitement and sense of urgency
- Motivate and engage others
- Reward action
- Inspire loyalty
- Encourage initiative
- Ignore or overcome constraints and barriers
- Negotiate win-win agreements
- Juggle competitive pressures
- Champion challenging projects
- Network internally and externally

SELECTING THE CATALYZING MINDSET AS A PRIORITY

Which organizational life cycle stage clearly requires the Catalyzing Mindset? It is the fast growth stage, where product launch fallout (positive or negative) and the opportunity to expand the customer base take center stage. This growth stage frequently resembles a hockey stick on a sales chart because of the sharp upward trend. This sales bonanza may flow from customer insight, innovative products, unfolding market opportunities, or the luck of being at the right place at the right time (consider the pet rock or Beanie Babies). During the growth phase, a "hot" streak, good PR, customer praise, outstanding reviews, and social media recommendations make all things seem possible. If growth and enthusiasm truly escalate, the challenges associated with new locations, franchising, distribution channels, licensing agreements or global expansion become critical.

American Online, or AOL, exemplifies how a Catalyzing Mindset jump starts a growth phase. The founder of AOL, Steve Case, learned from running a limeade stand in Hawaii that it was important to focus on the customer—a conviction he held as he formed AOL, which started with a spunky underdog culture. With its user-friendly content, groundbreaking flat-fee strategy, pervasive distribution of CDs to install, instant messaging, and aggressive marketing—including product placement in the movie *You've Got Mail*—AOL prospered.

In 2000, AOL's high stock valuation spurred the purchase of Time Warner in the hopes of dominating the broadband environment. After all, the sky was the limit, and any obstacle could be overcome. The trouble was a lack of due diligence. The growth-oriented Catalyzing Mindset of AOL executives clashed with the more established, risk-averse culture of Time Warner. The promise of synergies failed to materialize, and board tension eventually doomed the merger. AOL was later spun off as an independent firm.

Was the merger fatally flawed from the start? Perhaps. After all, the Catalyzing Mindset comes with its own set of risks. The desire for speed and a sense of invincibility distorts judgment. Similarly, a desire to jump on the bandwagon and follow "what's hot" can submerge common sense and realistic assessments. When growth comes too fast, poor decisions and blunders make the wheels fall off the bandwagon, and the parade grinds to an excruciating halt.

Keeping up with customers means holding user conferences, conducting meaningful customer surveys, creating reward systems that recognize good customer service (internal or external), measuring traffic at call centers, offering customer service training, and supporting rhetoric with system support and follow-through. It also means aligning energies,

[73]

negotiating, and encouraging others to meet customer requirements. Responses such as "It's not my job" are rejected, even when they might be true. When key customers are lost, service complaints mount, market share wanes and a competitor's product line grabs all the buzz. The Catalyzing Mindset should be used to revitalize the firm's standing with customers and the market.

AVOIDING IMBALANCES

A narrow focus on the Catalyzing Mindset for extended periods may produce bedlam, confusion, and inadequate systems. Certainly, the allure of spectacular growth is enticing, but it can also blind us to internal concerns. Growth must be supported by systems and capacity or it becomes a house of cards. Insufficient infrastructure to accommodate rapid growth, untrained customer service staff, and questionable quality practices wreck prospects and derail achievement. We must take the time to separate feasibility from fantasy.

Staying attuned to customers can backfire if those customers are the wrong ones; that is, they cost the organization more than they return if they are never satisfied. Not all customers are equal. Some expect a full refund for apparel they've worn for more than a year. Others expect too much "hand-holding" and yet others continually complain because nothing is good enough.

Similarly, an emphasis on just "getting it done" can result in shoddy work or high levels of stress. Likewise, an action orientation may entail costly returns or repairs. The impact on the bottom line suffers. High levels of customer dissatisfaction, employee frustration, and continual crisis management are also potential pitfalls. This type of problem reminds us of the Yogi Berra quote, "We're lost, but we're making good time."

Following are some indicators that imbalances may have set in.

There are culture-related problems.

1. Sound bites are mistaken for actual communication.
2. Negative stereotypes are attached to those who do not immediately "get on board."
3. Planning and monitoring are seen as distractions.

4. Results are expected too quickly.
5. Problems or disappointments are buried to maintain momentum.
6. Immediate action is expected in every instance based on the assumption that all opportunities are fleeting.
7. Instances of over-promising and under-delivering multiply.

Problems are ignored and positive trends are exaggerated.

8. System constraints are overlooked.
9. Details are frequently missed or slip through the cracks.
10. Decisions are based on exaggerated projections rather than reality.
11. Growth is confused with long-term success.
12. Benefits are overestimated and ramifications are underestimated.
13. Resources are stretched too tight for too long.

Human resources management is insufficient.

14. Staff is overburdened by unreasonable expectations.
15. Inadequate training is offered to personnel.
16. There is poor resource planning.

The Catalyzing Mindset may mistake sizzle for substance. If we stick solely to this mindset, we may become mesmerized by our own message and become convinced that all our ideas are destined for stardom. We may also fall for the "flavor-of-the-month" prospect and pursue it with unwarranted confidence. Other failings may stem from believing that fast growth will be sustained unabated, that market metrics and data do not need in-depth analysis, or that any problem can be resolved with additional funds for branding, sales staff, or additional advertising.

When the Catalyzing Mindset priority is out of balance, increased buzz about the company or increased traffic in stores or on the website may be equated with actual success. In addition, emphasis on an on-time launch may leave no time for rigorous product testing. Although the "test it in the market" strategy has worked for Microsoft as well as other tech firms, the failure to fully vet a product can be harmful. An early, but less-than-elegant, release of products or services can backfire, as it did for the 2013 Affordable Care Act website and for various state-level online unemployment systems.

The Danger of Merger Mania

The push for growth has led countless companies to acquire promising firms, make significant alliances, and license patents. In the rush to squeeze through a window of opportunity, companies may overlook important questions about their ability to merge technical systems, meld incongruent cultures and practices, restructure reporting relationships, and adjust staffing where there is redundancy. There may also be challenges related to creating new information channels, monitoring merger progress, gaining strategy alignment, and ensuring that available information on the new firm is comprehensive and accurate. Remaining nimble while growing is not an easy feat. Frequently, promising acquisitions are later spun off at a loss and with a renewed resolve to stick to core competencies.

Although hindsight is 20/20, we truly need foresight. We can conduct careful analyses to sharpen our understanding of the situation before we commit to merge, acquire, or invest. For example, Quaker Oats bought Snapple in 1994 for one billion dollars. On the surface, adding a fast-growing beverage firm to the existing food giant promised an expanded market. Unfortunately, the distribution channels between the two product lines were poles apart. Snapple sold to small mom-and-pop stores, not chains. Twenty-seven months after the purchase, Snapple was sold for $300 million—a substantial loss.

In 2005, the $35 billion Sprint–Nextel merger combined a consumer-based telecommunications firm with a business-based firm. Unfortunately, within two years, eighty percent of the cost was written off because culture clashes blocked internal synergies. In 2013, the Nextel brand was shut down.

And in 1992, the entertainment industry leader was Blockbuster, with 9,000 retail outlets after the acquisition of Major Video and Erol's Video. In 1999, Blockbuster went public and grew into a video behemoth. By 2000, income from late fees alone was $800 million. However, Netflix went public in 2002 and offered video delivery to homes: no more having to go out or return on time. In 2010, Blockbuster declared bankruptcy. One year later, Dish Network purchased and operated Blockbuster for two years. In 2013, all remaining stores closed. Within two years, the merger that looked so promising became a failure.

ASSESSING CURRENT CONDITIONS

How does an organization gain insight into whether the Catalyzing Mindset is being used effectively? First, it can assess the extent of reliance on that mindset for planning and decision making. Optimism is good, but it should be reality-based enthusiasm. Second, it can look at the broader climate, including customer relations, market position, and the alignment between action and motivation. To assess the climate, organizations must pay special attention to the following questions.

Customer Relations Questions

- Is customer satisfaction measured reliably and regularly?
- Are there multiple strategies to engage and listen to the customer?
- Are customer communications fully leveraged? Are they seen as distinct from PR?
- Are customer concerns/complaints handled efficiently?
- Are customer concerns resolved effectively the first time?
- Are people rewarded for providing good customer service? How much do the rewards increase with closeness to the customer?
- Do employees consider customer contact a disturbance, interruption, or hindrance?
- Are changing customer trends shared frequently within the organization?
- Is time allocated to share updates on customer concerns?
- Are there full investigations into instances in which customers are concerned as well as in which customers are delighted?
- Are customer growth goals balanced by other metrics that ensure long-term success?

Market Position Questions

- Are revenues growing?

- Is market share growing?
- Is the pricing, promotion, and product mix right for the market?
- Is training in customer service provided?
- Is technical and customer support easily attained to resolve customer questions?
- Are people who demonstrate a customer orientation slated for advancement?
- Is the firm leading its competition?
- Is our market position (leader, fast follower, slow adapter) sustainable and effective?
- Is the value of the brand fully understood and appropriately protected?

Aligned Action and Motivation Questions

- Does everyone understand the mission?
- Are people involved and committed?
- How quickly can we implement action or shift plans?
- Are we negotiating effectively?
- Are high performers recognized?
- Are people rewarded for results or for being busy?
- Is communication persuasive, effective, and timely?
- Do cross-functional and multi-disciplinary networks ensure customer satisfaction?
- Is performance monitored and managed effectively?
- Are people promoted based on accomplishments or tenure?

SHARPENING THE CATALYZING MINDSET

The Catalyzing Mindset encourages flexibility, responsiveness, customer focus, and market growth. If we elect to focus on the Catalyzing Mindset as a top priority, the following questions can bolster our mindset readiness as well as elicit good group discussions. The goal is to surface new ideas about how to enhance customer centricity.

Customer Analysis

Who are our key customers? This is not always as easy a question to answer as it seems. A new company may go into business planning to deliver its products to one set of customers and then discover that another group is also purchasing. Which group is really key to the future?

What attracts and retains our customers? Customers may find value in innovation, as with Apple products, or with lower prices, as with Wal-Mart. Firms that "lose touch" with customers can find themselves in a death spiral. Organizations must segment each of their customer groups and monitor them closely.

How can we grow our customer base? Markets are not stagnant, and staying up-to-date is critical. Advertising in print media served the broad market. But social media and networking influence specific customer segments. In addition to catering to existing customers, organizations need to identify non-customers and find ways to reach out to them.

Market Focus

Who/what is the competition? Competitors pop up from both expected and unexpected places. The Catalyzing Mindset must search beyond obvious rivals to spot up-and-coming contenders and determine whether new technology might permit an existing organization to become a key challenger.

What will it take to stay ahead of the competition? The answer is a moving target. Perhaps it will be faster customer service, new features, "rightsizing" products and/or services, loyalty reward programs, extended offerings, or higher quality products. Whatever it is, a company that outpaces the competition will thrive.

What additional market options are feasible? The "do it now" aspect of the Catalyzing Mindset must be balanced with a future focus. Predicting where new opportunities might arise, determining whether to move up or down market, changing geographical scope, and identifying new alliances are also critical to long-term success. Sometimes this might mean moving up the value chain or moving down it, or determining how to keep options open.

Operational Analysis

What will it take to reach our goal? Gaining support for implementation is a critical component of this mindset. The only way to fulfill expectations is to have systems ready to execute. Winning and keeping internal support means that schedules will be kept, invoices will be sent, and quality will be maintained.

What is our timetable? Getting things done and out the door fulfills expectations and builds customer loyalty. However, to keep things on schedule, timetables must be realistic and accepted. Knowing what it takes to deliver on time prevents any tendency to propose impractical time lines.

Who can help us succeed? In the quest for success, this mindset looks beyond titles, established jurisdictions, tradition, and established support to find new collaborators. Experts as well as novices can contribute if assistance is requested.

What will get people on board and committed? Initiative and discretionary effort stem from clear objectives, supportive systems, effective rewards, and up-to-date two-way communication. Engagement comes from giving others roles where they recognize they can make a difference.

What additional resources can be tapped? Knowing how, when, where, and who to ask for additional resources is key. Whether the goal is to upscale, reposition, or deal with surprises, there are times when unexpected situations necessitate new inputs.

Who delivers results quickly? Teamwork, collaboration, high performance, and initiative advance performance and results. But so do reliable suppliers, troubleshooters, and logistical support.

How can our responsiveness be increased? Factors include establishing early signals and metrics that monitor potential issues, recognizing those who have demonstrated alertness, conducting reflection sessions to learn from the past, and scanning for emerging needs and trends.

What ensures success? Pitfalls, constraints, product shortages, and weak commitment derail success. Systems to address emerging problematic situations can be installed. Knowing how to predict, detect, and react to any barrier goes a long way to guarantee success.

Whose support is needed? Too often, support is equated with those who can authorize or finance a project. In fact, implementers are the real key to making things happen. Working to win and sustain support from all corners of the organization pays dividends. If a crisis emerges, all hands will be on deck quickly.

When we operate from the Catalyzing Mindset, the desire for action may not permit a full response to each of these questions. We are likely to fall prey to the "ready, fire" stance as we strive to "get the order," "get it done," and "be number one." We sometimes consider that this is the greater good, and so we sideline planning, validating, and risk reduction. This mindset adheres to the idea that "those who say 'it cannot be done' should get out of the way of those doing it," but actual success also requires execution and follow-through.

SUMMARY AND NEXT STEPS

Adopting the Catalyzing Mindset as our top organizational priority means we elect to concentrate on customers, reputation building, competitors, and market growth. Customers are always asking, "What have you done for me lately?" Even if it isn't the organization's current priority, attention to customers and identifying market trends must be carefully monitored for a company to thrive.

Luckily, few stay totally consumed by the Catalyzing Mindset, which is smart. Mindsets must shift in response to our fluid environment. And, in order to continually provide outstanding customer service, we will require sound internal systems, clear policies, and appropriate capacity. All these factors dominate our attention when we switch to the Developing Mindset in Chapter Five.

Building Foundations
The Developing Mindset

If you built castles in the air, your work need not be lost; that is where they should be. Now put the foundations under them.

—*Henry David Thoreau*

A well-designed organization helps everyone in the business do her or his job effectively

—*Jay R. Galbraith*

Visionaries may dream up powerful ideas, but it is those who have prioritized the Developing Mindset who ultimately translate those dreams into concrete reality. When we employ the Developing Mindset, we concentrate on building a solid infrastructure, developing policies to guide action and creating clear accountabilities for lasting excellence. We recognize that operational issues such as work schedules, information flow, purchasing standards, human resource practices and policies, and financial monitoring underpin continuing high performance. This mindset subscribes to Aim Mutual Fund's slogan "Discipline creates performance."

WHY LEADERS NEED THE DEVELOPING MINDSET

Without tracks, trains cannot operate. People using the Developing Mindset make sure those tracks are built where they are needed and effectively integrated. They help design an organizational structure based on principles such as centralization, decentralization, networking, and using matrixes. These principles help delineate organizational roles and accountabilities.

Much as architects design buildings, we concentrate on the organization's "architecture" when we operate from the Developing Mindset. And, like an architect, we combine systems thinking, design, creativity, and a holistic perspective. Just as office buildings in Miami and Reykjavik have different construction requirements, organization design also varies by country, industry, location, size, product line, and mission.

The Developing Mindset has a long and honorable history, even making an appearance in the *Bible*. In Exodus 18, Jethro advised Moses to create a centralized structure with leaders directing ten, then fifty, then a hundred, and finally a thousand men. Today, organizations still struggle over proper "spans of control," trying to determine which configuration will deliver stability, predictability, efficiency, and consistency.

There is no one right permanent answer. In fact, many organizations shift between issues such as centralization and decentralization. Much like an accordion player whose music depends on compression then expansion, organizational leaders structure the organization sometimes with tight control and at other times with great autonomy depending on their circumstance. Whether it is contracting into centralization or expanding accountabilities with decentralization, form must follow function.

The Developing Mindset also digs into issues such as setting pay levels, creating reporting relationships, and establishing unit performance levels.

Leaders with this mindset weigh the advantages and disadvantages of different alternatives to create the best structure for their organization. It cannot be a cookie-cutter approach. It requires a tailored and integrated system for sustained excellence.

This mindset remains intensely interested in the need for effective systems, clear governance, and reducing the risk of things "falling through the cracks." Thanks to its macro perspective, this point of view identifies problems and impediments that go undetected by others focused on immediate concerns.

The strategic design aspects of the Developing Mindset are not limited to senior executives. Infrastructure issues appear at all levels. Mid-level leaders must organize work, provide clear guidance, delegate work to the appropriate level, and encourage the sharing of best practices. Entry-level positions reflect the Developing Mindset focus with their attention to job descriptions, performance goals, standardized processes, and reporting relationships. In essence, the Developing Mindset supports the philosophy that an ounce of crisis prevention is preferable to a pound of cure. Problem prevention may not have the flare of the Catalyzing firefighting mentality, but it offers the advantages of building a reputation for excellence, guaranteeing capacity to meet needs, ensuring timely communication flow, and erecting systems that cross functional silos.

Just as a sculptor chips away at the marble to reveal a desired image based on an intended design, our Developing Mindset employs a systems perspective to structure an organization for effective operations. Convinced that achievement will be maximized after clear and uniform policies and systems are in place, this mindset views organizational charts, goal statements, and position responsibilities as more than just pieces of paper. These documents are as critical to the organization as the skeleton is to the human body. The infrastructure supports, connects, and directs actions that enable success.

The focus of the Developing Mindset contrasts sharply with that of the Catalyzing Mindset. The latter focuses on external issues such as customers and competitors, whereas the Developing Mindset scrutinizes internal interdependencies and operational systems. But taking our eye off the customer does not mean that this mindset doesn't contribute to the bottom line. By ensuring that products get out the door on time and on budget, this mindset turns commitments into realities—and financial gain.

Issues such as levels of autonomy, information sharing, chain of command, seamless operations, and goal setting remain critical. These factors reduce the frequency of short-term crises and confusion while increasing the likelihood of long-term viability.

Developing Mindsets do not operate solely in the stratosphere. Some concerns happen at miles above the earth and others happen at 100 feet. Using this frame of reference, we consider the proverbial trees and the forest as well as other factors, such as terrain and weather. Those operating from this mindset make decisions and policies that are practical and impressive in terms of managing paradox, reducing chaos, and attaining results.

Our most admired companies pay continuous attention to internal structure, systems, policy, and capacity. The Developing Mindset knows how to anticipate thorny issues and recognizes that fire prevention is preferable to fire fighting. This mindset acknowledges unique requirements, builds specific strengths, and creates the policies and goals to direct decisions and action.

Do Not Underestimate this Mindset

Impatient leaders may wonder why they should waste time on administrative matters when it is the customer that counts, or why they should design organization structures and systems when change is inevitable. The answer is that just letting things "flow" produces confusion, rework, and crisis-management and, at times, the chaos that can destroy a firm.

You cannot ignore the lighting, heating, or electrical systems in a home just as you cannot ignore facilities, equipment, capacity, accountabilities, and workflow in an organization. In a home, these features may not offer the pizzazz of a fireplace or a kitchen island, but a house without working systems parallels an organization without effectively designed and integrated systems. Organizational systems do not usually create the same PR buzz as a breakthrough new product, but they create the foundation for news-worthy achievements. And the lack of effective systems can easily create negative headlines as well as increase overhead costs and tarnish the brand.

The Developing Mindset Knows the History of Organizational Principles

In 1947, the German sociologist Max Weber identified bureaucracy as the best way to organize a unit's function. He proposed that there should be a supervisor for every four to six front-line employees, an idea that was the benchmark for much of the 20th century. Weber's principles resulted in hierarchical structures or specialized bureaucracies. The fact that bureaucracy is stereotyped as unproductive today does not cancel its importance in establishing ways of dividing work and determining reporting relationships.

Since Weber's time, proponents of matrix design, strategic business units (SBUs), team-based organizations, and networked organizations have made it difficult to select the "best" organizational structure. Today, some organizations thrive with a loose SBU structure, emulating an entrepreneurial environment, while others succeed with a centralized approach. Some firms, like General Electric, have employed both.

Historically, organization size and revenue have been used to determine structure. An organization with less than $500 million in sales and/or fewer than 3,000 employees performs best with a centralized functional approach. Increased size, according to theory, necessitates decentralization by product line, customer or location/region. With approximately one billion dollars in sales, a project, matrix, or team-based organization becomes the norm. However, these simple guidelines overlook unique needs and the challenges associated with complexity and uncertainty. The goal is usually to create seamless systems and operations. Hybrids, networks, joint ventures, and conglomerates are among the effective choices for juggling demands of larger organizations.

FEATURES OF THE DEVELOPING MINDSET

The premise underlying the Developing Mindset is that investing in planning reaps substantial benefits later. Slowing the action may seem like encountering speed bumps to a leader functioning from the Catalyzing Mindset, but it actually paves the road to success. By focusing on resource allocation, reporting

[87]

relationships, and systems, the Developing Mindset ensures that the cart goes after the horse and heads in the right direction.

The acronym POSDCORB captures many of the activities that are central to this mindset:

- planning
- organization
- staffing
- directing
- coordinating
- reporting
- budgeting

As summarized by Peter Drucker, "A poor structure makes a high performance impossible." It's also true that the best structure in the world does not guarantee good performance. The following suggestions and examples illustrate the contributions of the Developing Mindset.

Lay the Foundation for Growth

Successful companies can frequently point to a leader who laid the foundation for future growth. In the case of USAA, a diversified financial services group, much of the foundation was laid by Robert Herres, who was chairman and chief executive officer from 1993 to 2002. He joined USAA after retiring from the U.S. Air Force as vice chairman of the Joint Chiefs of Staff and restructured USAA in a shrinking insurance market by diversifying product offerings and building a centralized information system function.

Evolve as Needed

Every organization is perfectly designed to get the results it is currently getting. The trouble is that most organizations want improved results, which must entail changing systems or structures. Consider the technology giant Cisco Systems. Cisco's CEO, John Chambers, initially organized the firm around customers' size and function (large firms, service providers, and small and mid-sized firms), employed a centralized research and development function, and outsourced manufacturing. Other infrastructure elements—including standard twelve-by-twelve-foot office cubicles, rewards tied to customer satisfaction and temporary staffing to meet demand surges as well as to preview potential employees—offered Cisco a high level of flexibility and predictability.

Among other things, the firm was noted for acquiring other companies and making the acquisitions work—not just once, but over and over again. The company walked away from deals if they did not pass Cisco's clear screening criteria. Their due diligence process examined cultural compatibility and reasonable geographic proximity. Cisco's fast-track acculturation system included a strong orientation program and milestone checks starting and continuing every thirty days for the first four months.

In 2001, however, the structure was changed to "councils and boards" to bring together cross-functional experts, empowering these experts to address complex solutions and entering new markets such as health care. It was hoped that this change would push decision making down the organization, reduce the level of redundancies, and expedite decisions.

Then in 2011, after several quarters of weak performance, the structure was again modified to more clearly focus on the company's vision. The new structure was designed to focus on five product areas:

1. Routing
2. Switching and services
3. Collaboration, data center virtualization, and cloud
4. Video
5. Business process architectures

Cisco announced that the changes "reflect a plan to improve customer, partner, and employee interactions, simplify its operating model and improve focus on priority areas." Time will tell whether these changes help Cisco stay ahead of the competition.

Remember That Less Structure Can Be More

Although the Developing Mindset is known for building frameworks, it does not have to be burdensome or permanently fixed. Sometimes less structure can be highly effective.

W. L. Gore & Associates is not only known for its waterproof, breathable Gore-Tex fabrics but for its radical structure. The company was founded in 1958 when Bill Gore created a team-based, flat, "latticed" organization with "no traditional charts, no chains of command, nor predetermined channels of communication," according to its website. The goal was to foster personal initiative. Instead of structural control, four guiding principles were established to direct action, including the following: fairness to all, freedom to grow skills and responsibility, ability for associates to make commitments, and consultation with others before taking actions that might affect the firm's reputation.

The firm empowers its associates—all owners of the company—to make their own commitments in regard to what they want to work on. As its CEO, Terri Kelly (CEO being one of the few titles in the company), stated in a 2010 Wall Street Journal article, "We believe that rather than having a boss or leader tell people what to do, it's more powerful to have each person decide what they want to work on and where they can make the greatest contribution. But once you've made your commitment as an associate, there's an expectation that you'll deliver. So there are two sides to the coin: freedom to decide and a commitment to deliver on your promises."

While not every firm can be effective using such an extreme form of a lattice structure, the Gore example does indicate that some companies can thrive with looser organizational structure.

Video game maker Valve Corp. is another example of an extremely flat organization. There are no promotions in the company, only new projects to work on. And compensation levels are decided by peer votes on who produces the most value.

Another unconventional structure comes from AES Corporation (originally Applied Energy Services). It has a decentralized structure with minimal headquarters staff and no strategic planning group, human resources department, or business development function. Multidisciplinary teams handle most of the work usually associated with specialists, such as choosing benefit plans, fundraising, and company safety. Prior to founding AES in 1981, Roger Sant and Dennis Bakke worked in a federal agency where they witnessed the problems associated with staff-driven operations. They committed to a flexible organization with as few constraints as possible, and the firm's revenue, profit, growth, and assets attest to their wisdom.

The firm views the phrase "human resource asset" as negative because it appears to equate people to equipment or inventory. Talent selection centers on general competence rather than specific skills. Believing that too many levels of management decrease an individual's desire to make a decision, AES has only five levels of management—and this is a corporation with 25,000 employees operating in 23 countries whose 2011 revenues were $18 billion.

Its reward system offers individual bonuses, plant bonuses, and organization-wide achievement bonuses. Internal promotions are the rule, and information is shared so extensively that everyone in the firm is considered an "insider" by the Securities and Exchange Commission. AES offers an example of how to create a unique design to meet specific requirements.

Even government organizations can be very different from one another. Within the executive branch of the U.S. government, practices vary significantly. The Department of Energy (DOE), one of the youngest federal agencies, uses six to seven times as many external contractors as the Department of Agriculture, which is located across the street. The Department of Agriculture is one of the oldest agencies and it relies on its internal staff rather than contractors.

Likewise, retailers vary in their use of centralized control. Although many create handbooks or manuals to guide decision making and action, Nordstrom provides one sentence instructing employees to use their best judgment.

Fill the Leadership Pipeline

When ITT appointed Harold Geneen CEO in 1959, it was based on his impressive organizational skills, his ability to interpret and recall data, and his ability to run a conglomerate of substantial size, breadth, and diversification. Committed to the concept that conglomerates moderate risk, Geneen purchased more than 300 companies in seventy countries. His ability to predict, control, and command was impressive, and so was the growth of the firm. When Geneen stepped down in 1979, ITT's structure was acclaimed as a marvel. Unfortunately, Geneen had not groomed a successor, and the structure he built could not be sustained. Like a sand castle, it collapsed, unable to continue as an independent firm.

In contrast, General Electric has placed a large emphasis on leadership development, which has helped it weather many challenges over the years. GE was founded in 1889 as the Edison General Electric company, and it illustrates how organizational design evolves through acquisitions, divestitures (light bulbs), and reorganizations. Its range of products progressed from lighting and appliances to finance, energy, transportation, aerospace, materials, cable news, and electronics. The product offerings continue to be shaped through decisions to exit businesses, acquire new firms, and organically launch others.

GE's extensive scope spurred CEO Ralph Cordiner to inaugurate an executive development function to build leadership bench strength and institutionalize change. This move has been cited as one of the key factors behind the organization's strong record of outstanding leadership. In fact, GE leaders continue to be recruited for leadership positions in other organizations.

GE's 2012 organization structure has six product divisions with centralized functions for public relations, business development, legal, research, human relations, and finance. However, there is also a centralized group, Global Growth and Opportunity, which stokes the organization's key growth engine.

Be Radical When Necessary

The Developing Mindset can embark on radical organizational transformation. After leaving the Reagan administration as Secretary of the Department of

Transportation, Drew Lewis was appointed CEO of the Union Pacific Corporation in 1986. Inheriting a hierarchy dating from the Civil War, he cut managerial levels from nine to five and gave field managers more authority.

To compete effectively, he also installed computer-controlled shipping and investigated train-control systems to increase rail capacity. When he moved the corporate headquarters from New York to Bethlehem, Pennsylvania, and took a more conciliatory stance with the union, the workforce recognized that the action signaled a significant shift. In the past, managers had unquestioned discretion to take disciplinary action at will. Although these changes were far from the last ones made at Union Pacific, Lewis' actions illustrate that a Developing Mindset takes on major change when it is necessary.

Be Wise and, Sometimes, Patient

There are circumstances in which the best response is *not* to launch a major restructuring or divestiture in the face of significant challenges. In 1993, Lou Gerstner became CEO of IBM and canceled his predecessor's decision to split the organization. He conveyed his confidence that the organization had what it needed to succeed in the high-speed, high-bandwidth networking environment.

Of course, this doesn't mean he did nothing. He actively pursued e-business service opportunities, diversified revenue streams, and developed new products within the basic organization structure. Within five years, profits, staffing, and technical reputation were restored. Deciding against the split proved wise.

Leverage Compensation and Reward Systems

Under the leadership of CEO E.T. "Ted" Kunkel, Foster's Brewing Group (now Foster's Group) encountered serious economic turmoil. Kunkel decided to create a more egalitarian structure—not the norm for an Australian firm—and committed to leveraging knowledge by increasing training. All employees became shareholders, even though the company had to give them interest-free loans to enable them to purchase the shares. People exchanged knowledge, best practices, and solutions to problems. Rewards were given for increasing personal knowledge, increasing productivity, and improving the stock price. This departure from normal brewing industry practices clearly worked for Foster's.

Kunkel was not the first to use compensation and reward systems with the intent to build a strong cultural foundation. In the U.S., Lincoln Electric engaged in groundbreaking practices; it was the first firm to offer paid vacations in 1923 and an employee stock ownership plan in 1925, predating today's ESOPS.

Other Features

In addition to engaging in many of the actions discussed, those with this mindset will often take the following actions:

- Increase predictability and reduce risk
- Set clear expectations
- Balance autonomy with oversight/control
- Design seamless work flow
- Create guidance/policy
- Craft smooth information channels
- Provide clear levels of accountability
- Identify goals and set outcome expectations
- Capitalize on talent and systems
- Transfer best practices and knowledge across the organization
- Construct effective monitoring systems
- Align team structures and tasks

SELECTING THE DEVELOPING MINDSET AS A PRIORITY

Whether your leaders, especially your executive leaders, should adopt a Developing Mindset as a top priority depends on your specific circumstance. For instance, is your organization losing customers due to chaotic internal circumstances? Is there evidence of confusion or "turf wars"? Is the infrastructure unable to keep up with demand? Do employees misunderstand roles and expectations?

If the answer to one or more of these questions is, "Without a doubt, yes!," your leaders should consider making this mindset a priority.

The Developing Mindset can, of course, contribute to success during all organizational life cycles, but it typically takes center stage following a high-growth phase. That is when gaps appear, crises arise, bottlenecks surface, and shortages become disruptive. Systems need adjustment and standardization. Consistency becomes critical. Leaders using the Developing Mindset may not produce perfect systems or remove all impediments to success for all time, but a new level of organization effectiveness ensures that they can build an organization's reputation.

In entrepreneurial businesses, the Developing Mindset targets ineffective, jerry-rigged operations and recognizes the need to swap chaos for more professional operations. In larger and more established organizations, this mindset becomes especially critical when there is a conflict between anachronistic traditions and new realities. This viewpoint addresses the gap between how things are being done today and how things *should* be done in order to prevent conflict, seize opportunities, and align resources.

AVOIDING IMBALANCES

Even if we correctly pick the Developing Mindset as our top priority, we must still stay alert to a need to shift to another mindset when situations warrant. For instance, we cannot ignore the potentially unpredictable innovation processes even when the focus is on seamless operations and "making the trains run on time."

We also cannot fixate on the Developing Mindset and keep adjusting the structure in hopes of finding the "perfect" design. Reorganizations take time and drain energy. Moving people around in the hope that it will kindle a sense of progress is mistaken. When we do this without clear observable benefit we are just "rearranging deck chairs on the *Titanic.*"

Frequent reorganizations lead to greater levels of confusion, lower productivity, and falling morale. Restructuring can provide a reassuring sense of taking decisive action, but it does not necessarily solve the problem or address an impending crisis.

Likewise, diversifications and mergers repeatedly backfire. Research studies suggest that seventy percent of mergers fail. Many disappoint because of a lack of attention to structural and system incompatibility. After the exciting blush of projected new markets and cost savings fade, structural problems often remain derailing promising alliances.

Kmart, for example, diversified by purchasing Waldenbooks, Builders Square, and PayLess Drug in the 1980s. The buying spree diverted attention from the established retail stores, which suffered lost traffic and sales. Attention to remodeling stores and building new locations in 1992 turned the tide, for a while. In 2002, Kmart declared bankruptcy emerging in 2003 with new investors. In 2005, it continued to diversify by purchasing Sears, expecting to grab market share against Target and Wal-Mart. A huge write-off, layoffs, and store closings followed in 2011.

Zeroing in on organization structure or acquisitions is only a portion of the Developing Mindset's scope. Operating from this priority, we examine whether staff levels are too large or too constrained, whether the reward practices distort individual excellence over team performance, or whether silos stifle collaboration. One key signal that there is a misfit occurs when there is a discrepancy between what the organization *says* it will reward and what it *actually* rewards. Many organizations may state that the retention of talent is paramount but then fail to make coaching or talent a promotion criterion. Overreliance on external hiring is another red flag that talent management policies require attention.

In another sign of imbalance, leaders may become infatuated with a particular structure, policy, or system despite evidence that it is leading to dysfunction or misalignment. Employees may be resistant to unrealistic schemes beneath a façade of polite acceptance, stalling progress, and reducing teamwork. If we follow the axiom "Form follows function," our plans will reflect reality rather than be detached from it in the name of an existing organizational structure. And even when form does follow function, the necessity for tailoring, modification, and integration remains.

Following are a number of indicators that imbalance *may* have set in.

Planning problems emerge

1. Top management develops plans without stakeholder inputs.
2. Analysis and planning replace action.
3. Planning is equated with producing an annual document rather than providing insights to guide decisions and actions.
4. Actions and requests are deferred until the "dust settles" from the latest change.
5. Long-term plans fail to offset high short-term costs.

Talent and culture issues go underappreciated

6. Talent is undervalued.
7. Competencies are outdated or inadequate to achieve goals.
8. Technical expertise is ignored.
9. Tradition or legacy is considered inconsequential in a change process.
10. The impact of change is discounted.

Systems-related issues receive short shrift

11. Systems design is based on existing processes rather than opportunities for streamlining.
12. Too much or too little is outsourced.
13. Narrow metrics overlook key success factors.
14. New system implementation is expected to be rapid, even though it alters work practices.
15. External "best practices" are copied without being tailored to the organization.

Attention is diverted from key issues

16. The customer and/or competition are ignored.
17. An internal focus diverts attention from new technologies or customers.
18. Communication flows exclusively downward and not upward or laterally.
19. Reasonable risk-taking is rejected.

JRRENT CONDITIONS

ɔn is a firm, agency, corporation, association, non-profit,
;hip, it requires a structure. After all, an organization is
ɔ. ɔup that agrees to be systematized, regulated, or configured to
achieve a mission and goal.

However, we may give insufficient thought to the importance of structure
and policy, because we become distracted by actual sales and operations. So,
how can we gauge the degree to which we are (or should be) focused on this
viewpoint?

First, we can review the factors listed previously to make sure we are on
top of issues such as the level of effective monitoring and control, information
flow, and policy formulation.

Second, we can check the broader climate—including organizational
structure, policies and effectiveness—in order to validate its match with current
needs and conditions. The following questions can assist with this assessment:

Organization Structure Questions

- Is the current structure aligned with the mission, customers, and
  stakeholders?
- Is the structure both stable enough to guide action and flexible enough
  to accommodate change?
- Is there a clear balance between the need for control and the need for
  initiative?
- Is the organization seamless? Are there minimal barriers to teamwork
  and collaboration?
- Is the degree of job specialization appropriate?

Organization Policy Questions

- Are the interconnections, networks, and teams effective?
- Is the number of managerial levels appropriate for effective oversight
  without becoming burdensome?
- Is performance managed and rewarded effectively?
- Are teams created and dissolved effectively?

[98]

- Is the level of risk managed appropriately?
- Are organizational and unit measures comprehensive, timely, and significant?
- Do pay and benefits compare favorably with others in the industry and locale?
- Are structures and systems reviewed, adjusted, and customized appropriately?
- Does information flow in an appropriate and timely manner?
- Are there appropriate external alliances, co-marketing agreements, or partnerships?
- Is the resource allocation process understood, monitored and adjusted effectively?
- Are capacity, facility, and structural planning appropriate?
- Are review and authorization processes clear and effective?
- Are extraordinary successes examined and key insights institutionalized?
- Are checks and balances established and effective at all levels?
- Are there sufficient controls for obligations, commitments, and contracts?
- Are best practices transferred across the organization?

Organization Systems Questions

- Are informal work-arounds supplanting formal systems and reporting relationships?
- Are outsourcing decisions effective for both the short and long term?
- Are decisions made at the appropriate level?
- Are internal systems—including information and technology, human resources, procurement, and administrative systems—aligned and effective for goal achievement?
- Are the reporting relationships and performance metrics clearly established?
- Are strategic goals guiding actions?
- Is knowledge collected and distributed effectively?
- Are employees engaged?

[99]

We use the Developing Mindset when we must provide clear guidance on expectations, when responsibilities are in dispute, when there is confusion about reporting relationships and when policy needs to be revised in order to support new strategic goals. This mindset constructs the backbone for facilitating work and ensuring mission fulfillment.

SHARPENING THE DEVELOPING MINDSET

Electing the Developing Mindset as our top priority indicates that our attention will center on structure, policies, and systems. The following questions can guide groups in creating the kinds of systems that facilitate growth, stability, and improved performance.

Systems Analysis

Generally speaking, what is expected of us? What is the plan? Plan milestones and metrics guide actions and decisions. Without a clear plan, there is a lack of alignment and a greater likelihood of derailment.

What is the best structure for us? Everyone may simply doing the best they can within a dysfunctional structure. Finding an optimal organization becomes critical to ensuring high performance levels and producing desired outcomes.

What systems should be established? Effective systems streamline work, speed action with timely information, and highlight both positive and negative deviations. As more systems are introduced, one of the key issues is how to guarantee that they are effectively integrated to reach current goals.

How can technology add value? Technology does more than merely improve communication. Employing technology across the organization to improve functionality will not only heighten efficiencies but also enable collaboration and timely action.

How should information flow? Reliance on vertical communication can slow and distort information. Lateral communication across functions and teams improves productivity, sparks innovative thinking, and leads to more seamless operations.

Process Focus

How do we balance freedom and control? This is a difficult and enduring question. Finding the appropriate compromise between extensive freedom to engage and enough control to ensure efficient resource usage, accountability, and compliance remains a constant balancing act.

What policies are necessary? The emphasis is on "necessary," because policies can become burdensome and outdated. At times, it is better to enable individual units to devise relevant policies, as long as they add value and do not establish unrealistic barriers or dangerous precedents.

How can we continue to deliver excellent results? This often boils down to effective planning, balanced metrics, and attention to execution. Specifically, enterprises benefit from monitoring processes in order to identify deficiencies and other problems early. This helps guarantee sustained excellence.

Culture Orientation

How do we sustain a reputation for excellence? This involves quality management, customer service, and both external and internal communication. It also requires a fast and comprehensive response to any crisis.

How will results be measured? Activities that get measured, get attention, and get done. Measures must go beyond outcomes and profit and include factors such as innovation, collaboration, system effectiveness, and talent development.

How can we resolve conflicts or crises? Simmering conflicts rarely boil over if there are clearly established goals, expectations, and resolution paths. Also, if we examine mindsets as the source of differences instead of assuming that differences are motivated by personal reasons, the number of conflicts will decrease.

Where can teamwork help? What level of collaboration is required? Team-based structures and practices often outperform individual efforts. Leaders must structure teams to match the task and delegate an appropriate level of autonomy to the team. A culture in which trust and respect is soundly established is more likely to produce effective teams.

What networks or links are necessary? Vertical connections alone are insufficient and tend to create silos. Such connections can also stifle innovation. Lateral or cross-functional networks must be established for effective communication flow and idea exchange.

What level of risk is appropriate? It may seem wise to avoid all risk, but companies that become too risk-averse miss opportunities. An acceptable risk is tied to the organizational life cycle and external circumstances, including economic conditions. During a recession it is wise to reduce risks, unless your competition has taken a leap forward.

How are core competencies maintained, developed, and reinforced? Everyone must accept the need for continual learning and commit to developing skills to handle advancements and remain agile.

SUMMARY AND NEXT STEPS

Whether or not we adopt the Developing Mindset as our top organizational priority, we must continually test, value and observe system and policy effectiveness. One key to long-term survival in today's marketplace is building a strong, consistent, and resilient foundation that remains change-ready. This does not happen by accident. It hinges on superior planning, organization, staffing, and coordination. It is not just a matter of "once and done." Relying on one design, system, or structure indefinitely invites dysfunction and distortion.

However, after the systems, structure, and policies are put in place, we must move the spotlight to refining, tailoring, and sharpening our practices. This improvement process involves a different mindset and a new series of questions, such as "How can we continuously improve our quality?" "What can we do to improve our financial return?" and "What can we do to improve and perfect workflow?" These are the types of questions reflected in the Performing Mindset, and the subject of the next chapter.

Measuring and Improving

The Performing Mindset

Measure twice, cut once.

—*Carpenter's rule*

Best efforts will not substitute for knowledge.

—*W. Edwards Deming*

The best thought-out plans in the world aren't worth the paper
they're written on if you can't pull them off.

—*Ralph S. Larsen Chairman and CEO, Johnson & Johnson, 1989-
2002*

Operating from the Performing Mindset, our attention converges on the
practical aspect of improving and streamlining work processes for maximum
efficiency and financial return. This includes improving quality, shortening cycle
time, examining inventory, establishing an effective supply chain, and reducing

waste. This mindset leverages data and analysis to improve practices and procedures with the goal of finding rough spots in the organization's fundamental infrastructure that require tweaking and refining. Our driving interest when employing this mindset is to remove superfluous or unproductive actions, install technological solutions, improve results, and prevent problems from arising. When we use this mindset, we concentrate on analyzing and translating data into meaningful information to gain keen insights into what actions will improve efficiencies.

WHY LEADERS NEED THE PERFORMING MINDSET

When we adopt the Performing Mindset, we elect to avoid the pitfalls of low quality or inadequate supply that might result in painful disruptions or tarnished reputations. The U.S. auto industry paid dearly when it overlooked systems and processes and could not match high-quality standards from international competitors.

Employing metrics, we uncover ways to adjust work flows, eliminate bottlenecks, and gauge efficiencies. Our attention to financial returns on investment, product quality, inventory control, and cycle time enhances our firm's competitive position.

Today's emphasis on "big data" and analytics particularly appeals to those of us employing the Performing Mindset. However, we must balance our attention to data based information with awareness of the dangers of "garbage in, garbage out" and narrow metrics. Otherwise, we fall into the trap of insular thinking and a singular focus on short-term efficiencies.

Operating with a Performing Mindset, we test assumptions, document and revise work flow, improve quality, and cut resource consumption. We also benchmark best practices for applicable ideas, ferret out existing new best practices, solicit input from frontline personnel, and explore performance obstructions; the focus is on excellence in all arenas. Similar to the Olympic motto "swifter, higher, stronger," the Performing Mindset strives for excellence in multiple spheres.

The Performing Mindset analyzes data and carefully calibrates existing practices for maximum efficiency. Without discounting the importance of innovation (Inventing Mindset), market realities (Catalyzing Mindset), and organization systems (Developing Mindset), the Performing Mindset considers data, information, and experience critical to the organization's success. It prizes quantified and qualitative measures as "more equal" than future projections. Data counts while trends and hunches are considered unreliable. This framework expects leaders to vigilantly track performance, fine-tune resource allocation, provide timely and meaningful feedback, and maximize both quality and productivity.

But data monitoring goes beyond completion metrics. Instead of being content examining past data, we require interim or leading indicators so that we can effectively make the mid-course corrections that guarantee on-time, on-budget outcomes. Recognizing that even the most well-crafted plan encounters surprises, unexpected bumps, and diversions, we closely monitor milestones and in-process measures. Just as NASA refines a rocket's trajectories mid-flight so it can stay on target, we recognize that being temporarily off-course is not a major problem. It is the speed with which an organization gets back on course that matters. Without timely adjustments, failure follows.

We should not link this mindset with the stereotypical bean counter image—it does much more than merely massage data. We use it to translate relevant and timely data into information that uncovers insights and solutions to emerging issues. Selecting and developing the tracking mechanisms that uncover early signals and problematic patterns offer substantial benefits, including:

- Identifying budding problems quickly
- Separating opinions and interesting anecdotes from significant facts
- Setting individual and unit performance
- Reallocating resources at critical junctures
- Monitoring and communicating current status and measurable progress
- Improving individual, team, or organizational practices
- Enhancing quality
- Increasing safety

- Clarifying accountabilities and standards of performance
- Reducing waste and/or warranty costs
- Improving cycle time
- Discovering insightful alternatives
- Managing the supply chain
- Increasing financial returns

Percy Barnevik of ABB, the Swedish-based engineering firm, observed that everyone has the same technology available to them. The critical issue is whether an organization uses it effectively. It is what companies do with technology that distinguishes the successful organizations from those that are a mere flash in the pan. To ensure that ABB used technology well across the 140 countries in which it operated, its leaders tapped 3,500 profit centers of approximately fifty people each to gain a local and granular understanding of what was happening with customers, competition, and internal operations. Each profit center had its own profit-and-loss measures to ensure it operated effectively.

Preventing problems, finding defects, and improving processes pays benefits. Electrical failures can paralyze a community, product defects can harm customers, and oil or chemical spills can harm the environment. Front-page failures not only are fiscally damaging but also devalue the organization's brand. Creating high-quality, safe products in today's turbulent and complex environment entails much more analysis than can fit on the back of a napkin. It takes careful planning to meet local requirements, understand each market segment, tailor procedures and processes, and deploy technology to remain successful. The following section describes the features of the Performing Mindset and includes examples that illustrate how some firms have effectively applied this mindset.

A Brief History of Organizational Measurements

The great management thinker Peter Drucker identified eight areas that leaders must measure:

1. Profitability
2. Market standing
3. Productivity
4. Innovation
5. Manager performance and development
6. Worker performance and attitude
7. Public responsibility,
8. Physical and financial resources to create a balance between short-range and long-range goals

Other measures have since proliferated, but tend to be variations on the same theme. For example, General Electric broke the term *profit* into controllable profits, incremental profits, earnings, and book profits. In addition, the company required multiple measures for evaluating individual performance.

W. Edwards Deming, Joseph Juran, and Philip Crosby brought renewed attention to process improvement and quality in the U.S. after the airing of the 1980 PBS special "If Japan Can, Why Can't We?" In response, quality teams proliferated, as did total quality management tools such as Pareto diagrams, cause-and-effect diagrams, check sheets, histograms, control charts, scatter-and-affinity diagrams, and systemic diagrams. Although success with quality management ranged from phenomenal to tragic, attention to analytics did not wane. Six Sigma techniques and reengineering remain effective management tools.

Attention to financial measures also increased with the publication of Kaplan and Norton's *The Balanced Scorecard* and Stack's *The Great Game of Business.* The balanced scorecard method uses four types of measures— financial measures, internal business measures, innovation and learning measures, and customer measures—designed to reflect the organization's true health and its ability to sustain itself. Clearly highly talented people and ideas are more valuable than items on a depreciation schedule. Although the value of sharing business information does not appear in accounting reports, ensuring employees understand the business's "what, where, when, why, and how" certainly facilitates effective execution. Today *open book management* contradicts the close-to-the-vest policy of assuming that information is precious and should be shared only on a "need to know" basis. Now we recognize that information fosters initiative, discretionary effort, and collaboration. Leaders must share both specific information and the larger context to provide the right guidance, at the right time, with the right measures and monitoring.

The concept of sharing information shatters the Industrial Age belief that equated information with power. At that time, information was hoarded and secrecy was pervasive. Production problems, market issues, and business opportunities were closely guarded and considered confidential. Today, the benefits of sharing information outweigh ego needs. The secrecy extended far beyond what truly deserved protection—for example, the formula for Coke. Even mundane matters, including schedules, were at times considered proprietary.

The opposite approach of sharing information bolsters innovation, creates seamless operations, speeds decision making, builds commitment, and smoothes teamwork. The practice of exchanging information also extends to suppliers. As bulletin boards display productivity, monitors display stock prices, and measures to gauge progress against goals are regularly and openly displayed, silos diminish, and outcomes improve.

FEATURES OF THE PERFORMING MINDSET

The Performing Mindset is paramount when it is time to improve systems and raise the productivity of the organization. Leaders with this mindset often adopt the following precepts.

Focus on Quality

In the mid-1970s, Xerox had a virtual monopoly on leasing plain-paper copiers to customers and collecting fees based on the number of copies made. When the business model switched to selling machines with technical service, revenues jumped. But the increased profits hid rising customer concerns with quality.

David Kearns, chairman and CEO from 1982 to 1990, responded with a renewed attention to rebuilding Xerox's reputation. He promoted a campaign described as "leadership through quality," which included the creation of a new planning process for products and services, the development of an information management system to survey the market, a top-down rollout of a 28-hour-long quality training program, the empowerment of employees to identify and correct quality problems, and a kickoff of the "Team Xerox" initiative. The latter was designed to improve work systems using more than 200 measures in key areas to ensure excellence. The large number of measures certainly defied the ability of one individual to monitor such a large array of data, but both hard measures and intangible gauges were essential to guarantee timely, relevant, and reliable information.

Metrics also help service-based businesses. Baylor Regional Medical Center in Plano, TX, is a relatively small acute care hospital with 160 beds and 2,200 employees. Yet, it performs within ten percent nationwide on key health care measures. In 2013, it achieved a 98.7 rating out of 100. Patient satisfaction was ninety percent, which exceeded national benchmarks. A retention rate of ninety-five percent places it substantially above national averages.

Governments also benefit from metrics. The city of Irving, Texas, regularly uses customer and employee feedback to achieve an overall seventy-four percent quality of service compared to the average thirty-seven percent for local governments. It holds an AAA rating from both Moody's and Standard & Poor's, an exclusive position that only 89 other U.S. cities can boast. Complaint resolution is also stellar. Ninety percent of all calls are resolved in the first call. Findings on the overall quality of life jumped from fifty-two percent in 2006 to seventy-one percent in 2012.

But Don't Become Captive to Quality Metrics

Under Chairman Robert Galvin, Motorola introduced the Six Sigma initiative in 1987 to improve quality and system performance. The goal was to keep defects to fewer than 3.4 per million. Six Sigma was a substantial challenge; the previously accepted standard in most manufacturing and service operations was 6,210 defects per million, or four sigma. Motorola's process improvement increased tenfold by 1989, and the company achieved Six Sigma three years later.

Motorola's other goals were to improve customer satisfaction, reduce returns, and slash warranty repair costs. Using the Malcolm Baldrige criteria as its guide, the company renewed its attention to latent supplier defects. Throwing down the gauntlet to suppliers, Motorola committed to working solely with those vendors that achieved Six Sigma quality. With a focus on removing defects from the process rather than fixing defects as they surfaced, Motorola improved customer satisfaction and employee morale while saving $3.2 billion in manufacturing costs in the first five years after launching the initiative.

Improving quality does not mean merely reducing costs. Improving cycle time and reliability goes beyond the standard cost-savings mindset. Motorola's cellular telephone operations reduced errors by ninety percent per unit, reduced part counts by sixty-two percent, and produced a tenfold increase in field reliability. Its pager division reduced total cycle time 300-fold.

Ultimately, though, quality could not sustain their market standing. Apple and Samsung swept attention and market share away with their innovative designs. In 2012, Motorola shed its mobile unit in a sale to Google for $12.5 billion. Two years later, Google sold it to Lenovo for $1.9 billion, while retaining some of Motorola's patents. This sequence demonstrates that, although each mindset adds value, narrowly concentrating on one mindset for an extended period can come at a high price.

Apply Metrics to Customer Service

Those of us drawing on the Performing Mindset can look beyond internal process improvement. Our focus includes analyzing external customer metrics to determine those customers offering higher returns, our ability to retain customers and warranty costs. Los Alamos National Bank, an independent community bank with 167 employees in 2000, is certainly not a financial behemoth by asset size. However, with sixty-six percent of market share and eighty percent of its customers giving the bank a "very satisfied" rating, it has plenty to boast about. Average assets per employee are $7 million, compared to its competition's average of $1.2 million and an industry average of $4 million.

Inc. magazine recognized it as one of 26 "banks they love" for its service to small businesses. It achieved this status by closely monitoring customer interactions.

Some firms embrace customer-centric data following a significant change. British Telecommunications, which had been a government monopoly, was privatized in 1984 and shifted from being a national firm to being an international firm under the BT brand. This shift required not only business-literate employees but, in a deregulated environment, a greater emphasis on results. Sir Peter Bonfield, BT's CEO, noted that customer service, innovation, and competitiveness had to replace stagnation and bureaucracy. Aware that success criteria had shifted, Bonfield oversaw the development of leading indicators, enabling the company to put the customer first, boost teamwork, and commit to continuous improvement.

Though at one time it might have seemed overly idealistic to assume that BT could succeed, BT defied expectations by becoming one of the leading international telecommunications companies. It shifted practices to target customer service through robust feedback mechanisms and effective data mining. Partly thanks to its focus on metrics, the company won the prestigious European Quality Award 12 years after deregulation.

BT also introduced a balanced scorecard framework in 1990, with the conviction that they could not manage what they did not measure. The company recognized that it was suffering from an overreliance on short-term measures, and it instituted more comprehensive and weighted scorecards to closely monitor performance across business lines and locations. In 1993, the British government sold its remaining shares in the firm. BT Group now provides international telecommunication infrastructure, including financial news and mobile voice and data services.

Link Metrics with Process Improvements When Needed

Prioritizing the Performing Mindset means we pay close attention to process improvement, not just quality improvement. Consider the example of Boeing. When it purchased McDonnell Douglas, its airlift and tanker program was struggling to satisfy one of its largest customers: the U.S. military. The government threatened to cancel the C-17 program because of cost overruns, technical problems, and late deliveries. To improve processes, Boeing replaced manager-controlled teams with empowered teams that were expected to function as small businesses instead of large bureaucracies. This meant involving customers and suppliers in the decision-making process and targeting eight process clusters. This coherent framework and open decision-making system combined to create a new "process-based management" practice that stimulated innovation.

The outcomes were impressive. One unit developed a dry sealant for fasteners used to assemble the C-17, replacing a time-consuming wet sealant process. With many teams improving operations, customer satisfaction increased from 75.9 to 99.8 percent. The unit ultimately received a Baldrige Quality Award, and in 2010 it joined Boeing Defense, Space & Security, one of the world's largest and most versatile manufacturers of military aircraft, with 68,000 employees and $34 billion in revenue.

Value Operational Discipline

We prize discipline and procedures when we adopt the Performing Mindset. The benefits of this approach are illustrated by Johnson Controls. Under CEO John Barth's tenure, the company developed an operational discipline that sequenced car and parts production so seamlessly that it eliminated the need to match colors as a process step. With that level of integration, the company became a supplier of choice, advancing market growth and revenue.

DuPont is another case in point. It defined operational discipline as a "deeply rooted dedication and commitment by every employee to carry out each task the right way each time." At DuPont, the term "discipline" applied to systems and process efficiencies that delivered more productivity, higher quality, less waste, better safety, and lower costs. Discipline was applied across the board, including housekeeping, complete documentation, compliance with procedures, and timely communication (including performance feedback).

But companies, even great ones, can slip. The Centers for Disease Control and Prevention's discipline faltered in 2014. Several mishaps resulted in partial lab closures to ensure the proper handling of virulent organisms and shipping errors also surfaced, demonstrating that even CDC's highly skilled and dedicated staff's discipline can waver.

Avoid Distortions of the Performing Mindset

Metrics must be carefully fashioned, analyzed, and installed. And they cannot be used in a vacuum. Consider the case of William Agee, former chairman and CEO of Morrison Knudsen. After his initial repositioning of the firm failed, he attempted to run the Boise, ID-based firm from his home in California. But Agee could not successfully lead from data alone, especially because some of the information he relied on included misleading accounting data. Data without context misleads and cannot be turned into meaningful information. Agee's overreliance on data hurt him and the organization. In the end, the board ousted him.

Al "Chainsaw" Dunlop is another example of a leader who, though seeming to focus data, actually misused it. His tactic of cutting expenses and reducing payroll served him at the expense of customer satisfaction and accounting standards. His cost cutting could not turn Sunbeam into a successful operation. His "Rambo in pinstripes" image could not hide significant problems and financial concerns. Dunlop was stripped of his position as strong concerns about dubious accounting and personnel practices emerged. Sunbeam filed for bankruptcy in 2001.

The public sector can also rely too heavily on incorrect, inconsequential, or useless numbers. The U.S. Department of Education measures the number of children in K-12 schools, the number of high school graduates, the number of dropouts, teacher-pupil ratios, and dollars spent per child. This is interesting information, but little of it provides insight into how to improve education practices. The number of students who can read at grade level, the number who mastered expected math skills, and the percent who display age-appropriate reasoning and writing skills provides more meaningful data. To be relevant, metrics must inform and guide decision makers.

And the data has to be inclusive—too narrow a slice will misguide us. In 2014, AOL's CEO, Tim Armstrong, referred to two employees' distressed babies as having cost their insurance firms one million dollars each. He cited this as the reason for changing the firm's 401(k) plan. Although his data was correct, the impact of his decision was totally unexpected. It took him one day to reverse his plans. He had overlooked his organization's culture and tradition while he was immersed in cost-cutting details.

Other Features

In addition to the features discussed previously, those who prioritize the Performing Mindset tend to engage in the following actions:

- Operate based on analysis or a "ready, aim, fire" approach
- Develop effective and broad metrics
- Translate rich and dense data into meaningful information
- Value both quality and efficiency
- Know how to identify redundancies, bottlenecks, and barriers to efficiency and how to optimize resources
- Track progress and adjust plans when circumstances change
- Identify performance gaps
- Improve safety
- Apply information from experts, experience, and best practices effectively

With this mindset, we find variations, deviations, and defects and then address them to ensure goal achievement. Quality, efficiency, and excellence are viewed as compatible and achievable. Though it's not an easy feat, we can deploy feedback, analysis and communication to align work flow, monitor progress, and attain goals. From this perspective, operating without data equates to driving blindfolded. It is reckless and dangerous.

SELECTING THE PERFORMING MINDSET AS A PRIORITY

Should the Performing Mindset become your priority? That depends. If your organization is undergoing a major upheaval, focusing on perfecting existing processes does not make sense. On the other hand, this mindset can become critical if your company already has an established client base and a set of products and policies in place and you want to fine-tune systems, improve quality, lift efficiency, and maximize financial return.

The Performing Mindset can contribute to success during all organizational phases, but it often takes prominence when internal problems surface. Business may seem to be going quite well, but when we go inside the organization and examine things in more detail, we find disruptive glitches, key customer concerns, outdated systems, poorly utilized resources, and an increasing error rate. The devil can be in the details, and the Performing Mindset will dig deep enough to find those fiendish facts.

Many organizations do not discover risks or problems until they elect to use a microscope to analyze operating practices. It is then they can find patterns, untapped resources and systems that unleash new opportunities and benefits. A major U.S. grocer, for example, examined 300 of its stores and found that 96% of their store-made cakes had anywhere from 1 to 32 ounces of extra icing—a costly and unacceptable variance. Another retailer found that excess milk spoilage stemmed from an ineffective bottle cap. Another firm discovered how to reduce the cost of plastic bags, reduce out of stock frequency, cut coupon abuse, and reduce signage costs after it scrutinized current practices.

Accounts of increased theft, safety problems, delayed deliveries, increased resource consumption, quality problems, missed opportunities, or lower ROI alert us that we need to analyze the details, so we deploy the Performing Mindset to reveal both opportunities and solutions.

AVOIDING IMBALANCES

Even if we elect to make the Performing Mindset a top priority, we cannot embrace it to the exclusion of everything else. For instance, a leader should not ignore potentially industry-changing external trends just because the organization is internally focusing on enhancing quality and perfecting processes.

We can become mesmerized by statistical information, because it is "logical," revealing, and bestows the illusion of control. Yet, data can mislead as well as inform. Even when calculations accurately depict reality, interpretations vary and consequences may have been overlooked.

Another risk is that we may be deceived by incomplete or misleading data. A customer service call center, for example, may focus on the amount of time it takes to complete a call but overlook the need to satisfy customers on the first call. Or a bank teller's performance may be deemed better when customer interactions are speedy, yet this single measure may push tellers to neglect an opportunity to sell additional bank services.

Imbalance can also surface when the "small" things consume a disproportionate amount of time and attention at the expense of the bigger concerns. An organization planning an off-site meeting with members flying in from all over the world spent four meetings over several days deciding whether everyone should have a two dollar souvenir. Focusing solely on "staying within budget" meant that only half the attendees would get the trinket, "saving" $200. Actually, eliminating several of these meetings would have been the easiest way to "stay within budget."

Like "gearheads" who tinker with parts and, after satisfying themselves that they understand how things work, leave the pieces disassembled in the driveway, we cannot be distracted by minutiae and miss critical interconnections or neglect to put things back together. Getting swamped in the details or falling prey to "analysis paralysis" sidetracks us from achieving our goals.

Following are additional indicators that an overemphasis on the Performing Mindset has set in.

Performance is hindered when:

1. Action is delayed until one hundred percent of information is available.
2. Leaders overlook or underestimate the need for new skills to implement new processes.
3. Managers assume data automatically sways support and commitment.
4. There is a search for a scapegoat when expected results are disappointing.

Poor data misdirects when:

5. The use of "averages" obscures key findings.
6. Most metrics focus on the short-term.
7. Leaders over-rely on quantitative or hard data without using qualitative information.
8. Only one metric, such as increasing shareholder value, really counts.
9. Reports inflate "revenues" or count them earlier than warranted.
10. Peak period variations are dismissed or ignored.
11. Leaders jump to conclusions based on partial or initial findings.

Decision making is adversely affected when:

12. Leaders extrapolate from historical data and ignore changing circumstances.
13. Transformation or significant change is rejected because it cannot be measured or monitored.
14. Leaders assume everyone sees the data the same way.
15. The importance of measurements being accepted as "fair" is overlooked.
16. Change or the need for new products or services is rejected because "everything is going well."

Important issues are ignored when:

17. Little attention is given to external change, including emerging issues and trends.
18. Most metrics define performance at an individual or unit level, rather than a systems level.
19. Human and cultural issues are discounted.
20. Tradition, goodwill, and reputation are assumed to be permanent.

21. The benefits of managed risk are rejected in the search for risk reduction.
22. Diminishing product life cycles are disregarded.

ASSESSING CURRENT CONDITIONS

There will always be room for improvement. So, how can we gauge the degree to which we should prioritize performance?

First, we can evaluate to what extent the features listed previously (in the Features of a Performing Mindset section) are evident.

Second, we can assess the broader climate—including organizational structure, policies, and effectiveness—in order to evaluate needs and conditions. The following questions can help with this appraisal.

Performance Questions

- What is our current level of performance?
- What constitutes best-in-class performance?
- What best practices should be adopted across the organization?

Measured Outcome Questions

- What will improve our financial position?
- What investments will improve productivity?
- How can we expand output?
- How can we improve operations, work flow, and safety?
- How can we enhance our competencies?
- What will improve quality and reliability?

Efficiency Questions

- How can we reduce costs?
- What is the best allocation of resources?
- Where can we more effectively use our resources?
- What will reduce rework?

- What will improve our response time?
- How can we decrease warranty costs?
- What will keep us on schedule and on budget?

We recognize that "what gets measured, gets done," so we must ensure that our measures are practical, helpful, and timely. And we must strive for a common interpretation of our information.

SHARPENING THE PERFORMING MINDSET

If we want to boost comfort and skill with the Performing Mindset, we can jump-start thinking about optimal effectiveness with the following questions.

Measurement Effectiveness

Are our measures derived from the customer's point of view as well as the organization's perspective? Both are needed for a comprehensive and balanced set of metrics.

Are the measures calibrated for local circumstances and conditions? Generic metrics cannot produce outstanding results. Frequently, they are so off-base that they hinder effective planning.

Are lagging indicators balanced with leading indicators? When we rely primarily on lagging or final measures, we are using the rearview mirror and trying to catch up. Real-time or leading metrics permit us to look forward. And the wider the range of indicators, the more effective we can be.

Are findings from customers, suppliers, employees, and performance metrics well integrated? Doing one thing at a time is now a luxury we cannot afford, and we must see one integrated big picture before we can finalize our to-do list.

Executive Focus

Do we measure all our major facets, including quantitative and qualitative aspects? Hard or quantitative information is only part of the puzzle. Qualitative measures offer a more complete picture, and we must let both "speak" to us.

Can our information systems provide useful overviews as well as backup details? If so, it's likely you already have well-integrated systems.

Do we use modeling, simulations, pilot tests, or intelligent experimentation appropriately? At times, the decisions we face have a level of uncertainty or risk that can best be reduced through the use of these tools. We do not have to "bet the ranch" if we can test the waters with pilots or experiments.

Are all levels of the organization committed to continuous improvement? Evidence of support from sponsors, analysts, and implementers is required to improve operations. Otherwise, islands of excellence will be swamped by poor systems or processes.

Are resources reallocated wisely to meet critical deliverables? There is nothing more frustrating for employees than to want to excel and start down that path only to find that resources derail their efforts and squash their initiative.

Are resources allocated for maximum effectiveness? "Maximum effectiveness" differs from "maximum efficiency." We must find an appropriate balance between the two for sustained success. Short-term efficiencies that subvert effectiveness can harm customer relations, sap energy and innovation, increase turnover, and diminish the brand.

Is performance monitored across units, products, and processes? Response time increases, enabling resource reallocation with coordinated and comprehensive data. Fighting fires in a noncritical area distracts attention from the critical gaps or problems.

Are problem-solving teams or task forces created to handle complex or critical problems? Many issues are complex and involve several areas of expertise, experience, and perspective. Getting the right people together paves the way toward innovative solutions and insightful planning.

Team Usage

Is team or individual feedback within their control? Useful feedback addresses issues we can change or are within our "line of sight" (i.e., observable practices or processes).

Are quality, project management, safety, and security practices continually updated and communicated? Finding ways to improve is only the first step toward actual improvement. New practices must be communicated, and, if necessary, training must be offered to ensure adoption.

Are project plan milestones sufficiently detailed to guide performance? Grand plans inspire, but only specific plans can be implemented. Turning the inspiration into reality is what counts—so specifics count, too.

Are best-in-class standards applied? Lip service to best-in-class practices is not the same as using best-in-class practices. Certainly some standards have to be tailored or customized, but the bottom line is that they have to be embedded into our daily routine.

Are site visits used to enhance high performance? Site visits or staff exchanges offer a valuable method for sharing what separates "the best from the rest." They also illustrate that the new practice is very feasible.

Are targets both realistic and challenging? Stretch goals engage the team, provide personal growth and ramp up energy. There is a fine line between keeping goals feasible and challenging. Improbable or crushing goals produce disengaged or demoralized team members.

Is data communicated quickly to every front-line team? Communication to all levels is critical to ensure change readiness and retain employee commitment.

SUMMATION AND NEXT STEPS

Though the Performing Mindset can produce a "lean and mean" organization, this can only take you so far. Many have found that you cannot cut costs for long periods and expect sustained success. The loss of key talent, market status, and agility is dangerous. After all, you have to retain the analytical skills and also the talent to operate efficient systems.

If these employees walk out the door, it's a costly blow to the organization. Therefore, a new need surfaces: one that focuses on people, teamwork, and culture. We must ask questions such as "How can we protect our culture as a competitive advantage?" and "Do we have the talent bench strength and succession plans for long-term success?" These questions reflect the Protecting Mindset and is the subject of the next chapter.

Cultivating a High-Performing Culture
The Protecting Mindset

Many of the things you can count, don't count. Many of the things
you cannot count, really count.

—*Albert Einstein*

There is always an easy solution to every human problem
—neat, plausible, and wrong.

—*H. L. Mencken*

When we operate from the assumption that employees are the most critical
ingredient in enabling organizational success, it is clear that the Protecting
Mindset is being employed. When we elect this mindset, we shine the spotlight

on creating a sense of mission, building confidence and commitment to excellence, fostering teamwork, and developing a cohesive committed culture.

Promoting skill development, collaboration, and teamwork sustains "spirit" and engagement. This mindset nurtures a sense of ownership that sparks discretionary effort and initiative. Here, our goal is to cultivate a workplace where individuals grow, support others, and achieve.

WHY LEADERS NEED THE PROTECTING MINDSET

The term *corporation* derives from *corpus*, meaning "body of people." If we prioritize this mindset, we elect to focus on people—as individuals, teams, or the entire workforce. Whereas the Catalyzing Mindset concentrates externally on customer satisfaction and competition, this mindset concentrates internally on workforce and culture. Assigning metrics to all Protecting Mindset concerns can be challenging, but it is certainly worth the effort. There is clear evidence that culture and talent are huge factors in an organization's success and survival. The Protecting Mindset bridges organizational boundaries, spurs collaboration, and sustains employees' energy with recognition and celebration.

These "softer" issues of the human resources arena are actually more difficult to assess than the more concrete factors and mechanics of management. Although the metrics associated with this mindset may be more qualitative, the outcomes are certainly quantitative, as the mindset is critical to market success and valuation. In 1975, over eighty percent of a company's value depended on its physical and financial assets, but by 2010, that figure had declined to less than twenty percent. Therefore, it is clear that employee skills and commitment contribute substantially. It can also be argued that the race for talent has accelerated this trend, with some firms able to recruit based on their standing as a great place to work while others struggle to fill their talent pipeline.

Successful executives attest to the linkage between spirit, discretionary effort, and success. The Protecting Mindset scorns a mechanical management approach in which personnel are considered interchangeable or expendable widgets. The notion that we control the staff with an on-off switch that can be thrown whenever necessary is false and probably delusional. Those entering the workforce expect a level of independence, attention, and involvement that necessitate a reassessment of what works and what does not. Aware of the complexity and importance of culture and values, we use this mindset to encourage growth and collaboration to serve both the individual and the organization with increased vitality and initiative.

While seeking to preserve unique traditions, we use this mindset to also explore new strategies and practices to maintain productivity, sustain loyalty, enhance knowledge, and build trust and confidence. We cannot be mired in the past with outdated assumptions about the leader's role, the workforce's intelligence, or the fact that internal collaboration beats pitting people or units against each other. Our changing workforce requires us to foster greater agility, resilience, and commitment.

For example, limiting authority and autonomy to the upper echelons was once considered sound policy. However, if we want true customer service, we must enable those on the front lines some flexibility, and when this flexibility is used wisely, we must recognize it promptly. What gets recognized gets repeated. The antithesis of this are outsourced call centers that greet customers with a lengthy standardized protocol, annoying the caller and handcuffing the service rep. A more effective operating premise is that the horse goes before the cart—that is, a talented and committed workforce precedes goal achievement and creates a unique advantage that cannot be duplicated. A dedicated and skilled workforce is a bulwark that protects against competitive intrusions. Talent has become so critical that firms sometimes poach employees—or even whole teams—from their competitors. The critical employee role is reflected in a non-compete employment contract. Intellectual property and patents not only produce income but stifle potential new entrants in the marketplace.

When someone puts workforce-related issues on the back burner, assuming that they are secondary or less critical to the primary business, they commit a fatal flaw. Although task and operational issues are important and visible, people count. Leaders recognize this and respond with coaching and engagement.

If people are viewed as disposable, we encounter workforce churn, a reduced ability to recruit new talent, and a workforce that merely complies with standards instead of discovering innovative solutions. Selecting this mindset indicates a willingness to focus on establishing and maintaining a culture that fits our mission, goals, and aspirations.

This mindset enables us to create stability in chaotic times, execute projects smoothly, and profit from workers' initiative. Like quicksand, which appears benign on the surface, poorly analyzed cultural change can sink an organization as trust and collaboration shrivel.

Going the extra mile to build a high-performing culture produces a competent, creative, and integrated workforce. But building and sustaining that culture requires careful planning as the workforce composition and required competencies change.

FEATURES OF THE PROTECTING MINDSET

This mindset creates and maintains our talent base and culture and deepens our organization's bench strength. Not only do we focus on building pride and trust, we also strive to remove unnecessary distractions and limitations that stymie teamwork, strategic thinking, and innovation.

Using this mindset, we assume that people seek growth through new and challenging assignments. Instead of assuming employees want narrow jobs in which they repeat the same work day after day and year after year, we shift our thinking to consider how most enjoy variety, change, and a sense of both making personal progress and contributing to organizational success.

Due to our inherent desire to feel proud of our accomplishments, we crave additional training, career coaching, frequent performance feedback, challenging tasks, and inclusion. This mindset recognizes the benefits of lighting a fire *within* people as opposed to the old nostrum that leaders must light a fire *under* the workforce to motivate them. An open, respectful, and engaged workforce outperforms one beset by fear and micro-management. A unified and aligned workforce is born from our free choice, not mandates.

When we prioritize this mindset, we often undertake the practices discussed in the following sections.

Establish a Unique Identity

Southwest Airlines' unique culture serves both its workforce and customers. Herb Kelleher, cofounder and former CEO, described his idea for a new type of airline service on the back of a napkin. He visualized a no-frills, low-fare airline with a culture that supports cooperation and fun. Kelleher was known for zany antics such as dressing up as Elvis Presley, donning chicken costumes at employee meetings, and hiding in baggage compartments to surprise flight crew and customers. Even the safety briefing at the start of a flight can be tailored by the Southwest crew. Laughter, singing, and contests characterize a unique and highly effective culture.

The culture is distinctive. How many firms have a "catastrophe fund" for employees who suffer a severe disruption in their lives? And this employee-centric approach is maintained with a culture where everyone is on a first-name basis, regardless of title or status. This informal and yet respectful culture is captured in the "people come first" strategy and the assumption that work should be fun, meaningful, and rewarding.

As Southwest's reputation spread, many cities urged it to expand into their localities. Kelleher rejected these offers, fearing that quickly increasing the workforce would dilute or destroy the culture. After all, the culture depended on hiring and training just the right kind of people, a process that could not be rushed.

When it did enlarge its scope beyond the southwestern U.S., Southwest maintained its careful selection process instead of relaxing standards. Its cooperative approach extends to its unions—it is one of the most highly unionized airlines in the U.S., with ten- and twelve-year contracts with its pilots' and dispatchers' unions. Although Southwest's casual dress code can be duplicated, its high-performance environment, which enables fast turnaround times for planes at the gate, cannot.

Southwest's success stands in contrast to the failure of People's Express. Both built a culture based on camaraderie and internal promotion. For both, initial success led many mayors to ask them to provide service to their cities, but only People's Express adopted a fast-growth strategy. They ramped up their hiring to accommodate expansion and in the process lost their special culture and people. Turnover accelerated to the extent that four of the seven original officers left the firm. In 1987, it declared bankruptcy, just seven years after its founding.

In an era in which performance requires discretionary effort, high skill levels, and commitment, performance management takes on a new emphasis and requires new approaches. In the past, some organizations thought that all they needed to do was set expectations, standardize practices, monitor performance, and then hold a steady course. But this strategy fails to spark commitment and initiative. Ownership, engagement, and teamwork don't come from a paycheck. Each individual decides his or her level of commitment based on how he or she is treated. Respect, trust, and fairness pack the kind of punch that an enforcement-style mindset can never match.

Create an Inspiring Culture

David Packard, cofounder of Hewlett-Packard (HP), displayed the Protecting Mindset with his statement, "Profit is not the proper end and aim of management. It is what makes the proper ends and aims possible."

Committing to a strong culture, HP's founders created the "HP Way" to stir innovation in the fast-moving world of technology. Packard was motivated by his experience of working for a large firm in which distrust pervaded the culture and employees had to sign equipment in and out each day to reduce theft. He concluded that lost time and low trust stifled creativity and overwhelmed any potential savings accrued from reducing shrinkage due to theft or fraud. Committed to a more respectful culture in which the workforce is valued, in the 1940s HP installed a groundbreaking employee health care plan. Later, it introduced profit sharing, open office space, "management by walking around," and flextime.

As successful as its culture was, HP also became an example of a company whose culture suffered after a merger. Following an unsuccessful hostile proxy war that was waged to "protect" HP's culture, the 2002 merger with Compaq became a reality. Ensuing decisions to lay off employees and increase the reliance on hierarchy took a toll. Shortly after the merger, the HP brand suffered, partially due to the dilution of its culture and traditions. In the past, HP's culture was seen as a type of "immune system" that blocked technical complacency. However, its traditions also may have fostered a resistance to change in some quarters. Success and a strong track record encourage some to hold on to the past or the "magic formula" that has served them well, but this can be taken too far. According to Buddhist teachings, the middle way of moderation is the sensible path.

Despite some potential disadvantages, most of us want our cultures to inspire loyalty, creativity, and commitment. Organizations as diverse as Apple and the U.S. Army tap the Protecting Mindset, paying close attention to tradition, retention, and strategic thinking to create an *esprit de corps* built on dedication, enthusiasm, and mutual support.

Reflect Important Values

Good values, ethics, principles, and standards promote pride, loyalty, connections, and commitment. An example of values in action is the Japanese camera-printer-photocopier manufacturer Canon. Its culture merges a desire for profits with a value system that strives for harmonious relationships among all stakeholders—customers, suppliers, workers, owners, government, and the environment.

As one of the first Japanese companies to institute a five-day work week, Canon forged a bond with the workforce that proved so strong that few strikes have occurred. Canon's culture extends to protecting the environment. It strives to reduce its impact on ecosystems, protect wilderness areas, and reduce waste as part of its commitment to the community.

ServiceMasters also focuses on values. Serving more than ten million customers through thirteen service-oriented subsidiaries, its culture has produced growth for almost three decades. In multiple years, *Fortune* magazine has named it among the most admired companies. But this achievement did not come from scrutinizing the bottom line. It is attributed to the firm's attention to delighting customers, doing the right thing, caring about people, valuing teamwork, doing "what we say we'll do," valuing diversity, committing to being a learning organization, and dedicating itself to innovation. It also stresses the individual's dignity and worth and everyone's desire to grow and achieve.

Of course, any firm can publish an exemplary list of values. Enron compiled a fantastic values statement. The hard part is living up to those values day after day, which Enron famously failed to do. We must "walk the talk" before we can say that we operate based on our values.

Celebrate Traditions

The Walt Disney Company is known for fun, movies, and a strong culture. Founder Walt Disney stated that "you can dream, create, design, and build the most wonderful place in the world, but it requires people to make the dream a reality." The "magic" associated with Disney hinges largely on the excellent recruitment and training of "cast members" (i.e., employees). Knowing that seventy percent of visitors to Disney theme parks are repeat visitors, the company provides a clean, friendly, and enjoyable experience. Though that may sound simple, it is a challenge when dealing with 34 unions, hot sticky weather, and large crowds.

Disney thoroughly screens applicants and onboards new employees with an orientation program called "Traditions." This program highlights the company's culture and history, providing a context for the company's organizational policies and standards. In addition, specific training programs help cast members develop requisite skills; frequently, cast members are allowed to develop their own work rules.

Disney uses stories to convey its values and expectations to cast members. Disney University was one of the first corporate universities, with an unusual twist—it did not have a single course that focused on quality in the curriculum. Instead, quality was incorporated into the whole program, demonstrating its role as a core value.

Disney is not alone in understanding how values and tradition spur performance and pride. The military has long understood that tradition breeds excellence, which could never be achieved through mandates, performance standards, or metrics. Troops literally sacrifice their lives for team members. Values also play a central role at Johnson & Johnson, whose credo stresses patient care first, respect for employees second, community service third, and stockholders last.

As organizations understand what it takes to both survive and thrive, new attention is being given to coaching, the ability to transfer knowledge across the organization, and the ability to build a common mission with valued traditions. When we align expectations, perceptions, and culture, we avoid pitfalls, gain support, and sustain commitment.

Be Wary of Corrosive Practices

A firm's culture can corrode performance and spirit. In fact, it can become destructive. Like sinkholes that hide beneath the surface, corrupt cultural practices can spread over time until they produce a cave-in. We must respond quickly when values are distorted or violated, when commitments are ignored, when trust is breached, and when legal mandates are skipped over.

Consider the mid-priced restaurant chain Denny's, the prominent brand of the Advantica Restaurant Group. In 1993, a CBS news story recounted the experience of several African-American Secret Service agents who were denied service at a Denny's. The story exploded in the media and grew as additional instances of service denial were reported. The restaurant's reputation suffered as late-night jokes and cartoons publicized the senseless treatment.

In response, James Adamson, chairman and CEO of Advantica, acted decisively. He announced that any employee who practiced discrimination would be dismissed. He said that any manager who disagreed with that policy should resign. The call for resignations extended to the twelve-member top management team. A year later, only two women remained on the top team. In addition, Denny's removed three layers of management, remodeled stores, increased the number of ethnic-minority managers, and introduced a new slogan, "New Day at Denny's." A cultural makeover had started. A Denny's customer survey was also inaugurated to allow management to stay abreast of emerging issues. A turnaround was achieved, reflected in a new employee workforce that is fifty percent ethnic minority and forty-two percent of franchises being minority-owned. In 2001, *Fortune* magazine recognized it as a Best Company for Minorities employer.

The importance of culture has often been overlooked when organizations merge or acquire another firm. When the "more equal" firm considers its way superior, it sows the seeds of not only tension but disruption. Culture can swamp carefully negotiated plans, anticipated synergies, and financial projections. With half of mergers failing, cultural planning must be carefully crafted and integrated into any merger analysis and design. As Peter Drucker stated, "Culture eats strategy for breakfast."

When Daimler merged with Chrysler, for example, the anticipated synergy between the two companies failed to emerge amid miscommunications and misaligned expectations. There were culture clashes between the centralized, hierarchical German firm and the flatter, less structured, and more risk-taking U.S. company. This "merger of equals" began to seem less equal as more Daimler executives transferred to Chrysler to reinforce Daimler's operating practices and culture. Ultimately, this lack of cultural alignment failed everyone. DaimlerChrysler's CEO Jurgen Schrempp asked, "What happened to the dynamic can-do cowboy culture I bought?" Over time, Chrysler became a subsidiary rather than an equal partner and in 2014 was sold to Fiat.

Rely on Uncommon Sense

We frequently adopt the Protecting Mindset when uncommon events or a crisis require unconventional actions. Take the response of Malden Mills CEO Aaron Feuerstein as an example. He was distributing year-end bonuses to company employees at his 1995 holiday party when he was informed that the mill was burning. Everyone left and headed to the mill to discover the main building destroyed. Employees anticipated a dismal holiday until Malden announced that he would continue to pay all 2,400 employees their salaries plus health benefits until production could be restored. Within approximately ninety days, Malden Mills was producing its Polartec fleece at full capacity and at improved levels of quality and productivity. This was an extraordinary recovery inspired by an exceptional decision.

Although a less dramatic example, IKEA also uses unconventional practices. The founder, Ingvar Kamprad, began the practice of packing furniture as "flat parcels," which requires the customer to complete the final assembly, but the company is also known for "penny pinching," corporate responsibility, and environmental awareness. The Swedish firm was the first to join UNICEF's Children's Rights Project in India. It also joined Greenpeace's campaign for sustainable forestry, agreeing to purchase only timber from sustainable forests. Efforts did not end there. The firm holds an energy savings competition and uses extensive alternative energy resources. Relying on these guiding principles, the firm grew into a leading and internationally recognized retailer.

IKEA offers quality at a low price, adhering to a pro-consumer philosophy, with empowered teams producing a steady stream of appealing new products.

The customer-centric approach results in tailored product lines for different cultures. For example, U.S. customers looking for bedding cannot fathom what a "160-centimeter" bed means. Instead IKEA offers standard U.S. sizes, such as king, queen, and twin. IKEA meets local customer expectations despite being a European company. Week-long training for franchisees ensures that the culture is maintained, despite some customization for local needs.

Don't Lose Your Balance

Prioritizing a Protecting Mindset does not mean protecting the status quo at all costs. Cultures must change to remain relevant. Organizations can sometimes miss the boat by holding on too tightly to everything in their past.

In 1984, the famed AT&T monopoly ended. At the time, its culture tended to have an internal focus and an employment-for-life culture. While its research arm, Bell Labs, invented many promising devices, including the transistor, AT&T remained preoccupied with providing land-based communication and failed to commercialize the discoveries. Geography also reflected the company's less-than-enthusiastic attitude toward change—Bell Labs was isolated from headquarters. The company was seen as the best in its industry and employees enjoyed high levels of pride, so change was seen as unnecessary and likely to reduce quality. Changing gears is not easy.

After deregulation, the company's market share sank and prices dropped. It became clear that it could not keep change at bay. Morale suffered with the loss of stature, and several rounds of layoffs and office closings sapped confidence. The old motto, "Our Employees Are Our Most Valued Asset," rang hollow for the 300,000 employees who lost their jobs. A sixty percent reduction in the price of long-distance service compelled change and mandated a new culture centered on customer satisfaction.

Workforce discomfort was high. Old practices, such as basing promotions on tenure, evaporated. Now, performance mattered. AT&T began to bundle its services, including online services, access to entertainment, and wireless services. This was quite a shift from the past, when for years the company overlooked customer preferences and only offered black phones. Torn by several transition efforts, AT&T wound up being acquired by the Southwestern Bell Corporation, which adopted the famed AT&T name.

Do the Right Things Because They Are Right

The Protecting Mindset emphasizes ethics as a key component of a high-performing culture. Going beyond legal compliance, the ethical aspect of the Protecting Mindset scrutinizes the level of honesty, loyalty, respect, and integrity that drives behavior and action.

This aspect of the Protecting Mindset has become even more important since the 2008-2009 financial crisis, which some experts have attributed, at least in part, to a larger culture of questionable ethics. In fact, some observers believe ethical problems can be traced back to the type of short-term thinking encouraged in many business schools. *US News and World Report* notes, "Peddling mortgage loans to credit-poor borrowers and betting on a sure-to-pop housing bubble may have paid off in the years leading up to the financial crisis—and boosted the stock prices of many firms run by people with M.B.A.'s—but they ended up being both harmful to the economy at large and losing strategies for those firms."

But ethics issues go beyond the repercussions of the Great Recession. Even in relatively good economic times, attention to conflicts of interest, résumé inflation, flagrant nepotism, discrimination, abusive treatments, social and environmental concerns, and health and safety problems lead to an increased awareness of ethical issues. Paul Wolfowitz resigned as president of the World Bank after his acknowledged romantic relationship with a subordinate created a conflict of interest due to his handling of her promotion and pay package. Scott Thompson's deceptive résumé created a furor until he resigned as president of Yahoo. Beechnut's practice of using less-than-pure apple juice in their drink boxes appeared dishonest, while Nike's use of sweatshops in its offshore manufacturing practices came under fire.

Although the discussion becomes controversial, some experts believe that certain global business practices have ethical consequences. The current practice of inversion—or U.S. firms buying foreign companies and relocating their headquarters to foreign soil to save paying U.S. taxes—is legal but considered by some to be unethical and disloyal. In the first half of 2014, Chiquita, Applied Materials, Medtronic, and Walgreens announced that they were considering such moves. And several other companies executed inversions to become non-U.S. firms subject to lower corporate tax rates. Reaction has been so strong that new legislation to curtail the practice is being proposed.

Other Features

These examples skim the surface of the concerns this mindset targets. Other concerns of the Protecting Mindset include:

- Encourage employee initiative and responsibility
- Build effective team practices
- Release creative and productive energies through increased respect and autonomy
- Recognize the impact of community, individual pride, and fairness on performance
- Encourage cross-training for increased flexibility
- Develop talent and offer coaching and career development
- Encourage the flow of information along multiple channels
- Provide creative safety nets for innovation
- Develop effective personal and professional networks
- Handle conflict effectively
- Create lateral networks, bolstering creative thinking and collaboration
- Implement talent retention and succession planning
- Offer developmental opportunities and expand competencies
- Ensure that reward systems are aligned to strategy

Although many of these actions are considered "soft," we all know that the soft stuff can be difficult. "Hard" business aspects include finance, engineering, and operations, which tend to have clear answers, well-tested solutions, and opportunities to run pilot programs to investigate results. Dealing with people is not a science but an art, and one that can be trying, since—even if we use the same formula, approach, or solution uniformly—skepticism delays responses and the results vary.

SELECTING THE PROTECTING MINDSET AS A PRIORITY

Should we prioritize the Protecting Mindset now? As always, the safest answer is "it depends," but there are some clear signals to watch for. For example, the Protecting Mindset should be considered if there are signs of "turf wars" within the organization. This mindset can be used to align energies and reduce internal tensions among different groups. It should also be considered when new skills are required to implement new strategies or goals. Since high ethics and supportive culture are key attractions for skilled employees, we will need to adopt this mindset if we struggle to hire talent.

Sustaining commitment is more challenging because of variance in perception, experience, and expectations. Just consider the generational difference in perspective on performance feedback: Baby Boomers are content with annual performance reviews, while Millennials expect feedback almost on a weekly basis. Higher levels of performance can be produced through this mindset's concentration on teamwork, employee relations, succession planning, appropriate autonomy, and commitment. These features are hard to ignore or forego.

Being among the "best places to work" or having a good reputation translates into an ability to attract and retain talent. It is not a matter of having lenient policies or providing unique perks, such as allowing pets at work or having a dry cleaner on-site. It is how it treats employees that makes an organization a fantastic place to work. Giving others the opportunity to grow their careers and feel that they make a contribution generally breeds long-term success.

We use this mindset to change subpar work environments, help those facing substantial change (technology, market, or regulatory), and establish new levels of excellence.

AVOIDING IMBALANCES

When we elect the Protecting Mindset as our top priority, we can get swallowed by the opportunities to refine, rebalance, and tinker with culture, communication, and cooperation. However, we must remain alert to the need to adjust mindsets when circumstances change.

Both U.S. and Japanese automobile firms had to make a difficult shift when quality problems necessitated large recalls. Faced with embarrassing problems, they had to refocus on quality. And they recognized that these quality problems stemmed from deficiencies in their culture.

A supremely confident mentality may have swept problems under a rug. Overreliance on hierarchical structure may have stifled information flow. Or a sense of invincibility may have resulted in denial that problems existed. When we use this mindset, we recognize that unproductive or distorted culture can be dangerous. We may be holding on to outdated practices that propagate ineffective norms.

As we employ this mindset, we must consider which aspects of the culture are outmoded and which add value. Culture change is an intensive and lengthy process, and keeping some elements of the culture stable smoothes concerns and facilitates progress. We just need the wisdom to know what we must change and what we should retain. "Throwing the baby out with the bathwater" rouses resistance. Certainly, there are aspects associated with tradition that we can retain as we implement a more effective culture. Attention to emerging signs that dysfunction has crept into the culture is much easier to handle than having to initiate a wholesale cultural change.

A productive culture can morph into a dysfunctional one. The following indicators raise a warning flag that things are slipping.

Change management and cultural monitoring is discounted

1. There is a reliance on formal downward communication and old metrics.
2. The organization relies on outdated norms and practices.

3. Management ignores concerns and trends, thinking they are passing fads.
4. Managers assume that change management is unnecessary, relying on their ability to implement changes in short order.
5. The past and present are seen in idyllic terms.
6. Little importance is attached to strategic thinking and management.

There is resistance to innovation

7. New ideas are quickly shot down.
8. There is a general failure to reward innovation or support creative thinking.
9. There is a rush to action, overlooking the need to identify alternatives.
10. The organizational bureaucracy stifles lateral communication.
11. Red tape, unnecessary levels of approvals, and hierarchy slow decision making and engagement.
12. Conflict is ignored and/or established rules and regulations are used to "resolve" issues.

There is a lack of information

13. Leaders tolerate information distortion and "yes-man" behavior.
14. Only a small group is involved in decision making.
15. Information is hoarded because an "information is power" mentality persists.
16. People who communicate potential problems are viewed as troublemakers and are censored.
17. Communication content shifts by the level of the audience.

Conflicts are not addressed

18. Leaders allow turf battles, hoping that competition will be good for employees.

19. A lack of cooperation is overlooked to avoid "starting a fight" or being seen as a troublemaker.
20. Loyalty to a leader or unit is valued more than resolving differences.

Reliance on favoritism rather than merit

21. Promotions are based on favoritism rather than on performance.
22. Performance metrics are incomplete, outdated, and/or unfair.
23. Social connections and visibility trump achievement.

There are other signs of dysfunction

24. Tradition and internal politics block the ability to identify emerging issues.
25. Competencies are not being maintained or developed.
26. There is a failure to plan for succession.
27. Asking questions and expressing concerns are viewed as "resistance."
28. There is a conviction that culture cannot be changed.

ASSESSING CURRENT CONDITIONS

Should you make the Protecting Mindset a top priority? One way to gauge the need is to evaluate current effectiveness, the environment, and potentials for improvement, as described earlier in this chapter.

Another option is to critically analyze the broader organizational and competitive climate—including culture, benefits packages, retention rate, satisfaction levels, engagement, and other factors—in order to decide whether this mindset *needs* attention. The following questions can help with this assessment.

Culture Questions

- Does our culture serve all interests?
- Do we "walk our talk" and live our values every day?
- Do we consistently demonstrate integrity and ethics?
- Are we alert to potentially rigid or negative aspects of our culture?
- Is high performance recognized and rewarded at the individual, team, and/or enterprise levels?
- Do we engage others in the decision-making process?
- Has fear been driven out of the organization?

Talent Questions

- Is our voluntary turnover rate acceptable?
- Do we implement a solid retention and succession plan?
- Do we have sufficient transfer of knowledge and knowledge-sharing?
- Are we developing talent for our future?
- Do we have a strong leadership pipeline?
- Are people being appropriately coached and developed?
- Are new competencies, skills, or talents being developed?
- Do we involve the right talent in decision making?

Team and Network Questions

- Do we have an effective level of collaboration and teamwork?
- Do we have sufficient lateral networks?
- Do we reap the benefits of cross-functional collaboration?
- Do we reward collaboration?

Communication Questions

- Is communication operating in all directions: up, down, and laterally?
- Is communication timely, trusted, and reliable?
- Is conflict handled effectively and in a timely manner?
- Are there performance distractions or blockages?
- What communication networks can be created or enhanced?

Policy and Plan Questions

- Are our policies fair and fully implemented?
- Are proposed actions or plans consistent with our culture, traditions, mission, and values?
- Do we review and revise policies and practices when events warrant?

In the process of checking these questions, we may discover opportunities to enhance our culture, change policies to boost performance, spur innovation, or develop workforce talent for the future through the Protecting Mindset lens.

Failing to Find the Right Balance

Business history is filled with examples of companies that maintained the Protecting Mindset as their top priority for far too long. In some cases, they did this in the hopes of keeping their workforces productive and happy. In other cases, they simply suffered from a sense that they were invulnerable. One of those stories is that of the *Encyclopedia Britannica*.

Published in Scotland in 1768, it was the first English-language encyclopedia. Purchased by Sears, Roebuck & Company in 1920, the company moved its headquarters from Edinburgh to Chicago. With periodic revisions and brand extensions (atlases and yearbooks), the *Encyclopedia Britannica* served students for generations. Sold by a direct sales force that targeted middle-income families, *Britannica's* sales reached their peak in 1989, when it dominated the market. A strong culture based on world-renowned experts and a strong sales force created a mindset that was, unfortunately, set in stone.

The organization's leaders rejected the notion that the 1993 *Encarta* product, an encyclopedia stored in a CD-ROM format, changed their reality. After all, that product did not have their experts preparing the selections, so it was plainly inferior in their eyes. There were cultural and motivational reasons for this shortsightedness. Their direct sales force was highly regarded for both their expertise as well as their results. Changing their product would mean that this valued sales force would have to forego their standard $500 per set commission, and the loss of their sales team. It was also hard for them to believe that an encyclopedia that could be bought in a grocery store could compete with their prestigious brand.

Company leaders knew that encyclopedias were opened only once a year after the initial ownership experience, and they knew that parents purchased the $1,500 sets to help with their children's education. It was an investment in their future. Yet they failed to recognize that parents' new major "educational" purchase was now the personal computer, not the encyclopedia.

In 1995, with an eighty percent loss in sales, the company was put up for sale. Software, media, and information firms all declined to purchase it. It was sold in 1996 for half of book value, and the new owners had a different strategy. The new *Britannica* became an Internet portal to high-quality reliable material. It relies on its brand name's connection to value, objectiveness, and accuracy and operates on a new distribution model, independent of a direct sales force.

SHARPENING THE PROTECTING MINDSET

By focusing on development, initiative, involvement, recognition, and teamwork, this mindset builds trust and confidence in the organization's fairness and its future. And with effective multi-directional communication, new ideas are both solicited and encouraged. The open exchange ensures continuity and aligns talents and decisions with current realities.

So how do you bolster this mindset? The following questions can help improve practices and invigorate the culture. Of course, the most effective actions complement external realities, existing conditions, and strategic plans.

Culture Focus

Do we constantly boost our unique identity and esprit de corps? Employees' sense of purpose and community are key to productivity. Bolstering this sense cannot be considered a "one-and-done" activity; it must be nurtured to be sustained. Otherwise, entropy will grind it down.

Do our decisions and actions support our culture? The organization's vision, mission, and guiding principles should guide action at all levels. And everyone should know how to respond if it appears that action might stray from these bedrock principles.

Are teamwork and cooperation rewarded? High-functioning teams—even those that work remotely or communicate digitally—maximize productivity, innovation, engagement, and commitment. Without recognition, performance slips, so we must reward collaborative teams as well as individuals.

Are people treated with respect? Employees disengage or voluntarily leave their jobs if they do not feel respected and appreciated, especially by their immediate supervisor. Too often mediocre performance stems from a perceived lack of respect and trust.

Are differences valued and encouraged? Diversity of ideas and perspectives produces better decisions and allows employees to avoid jumping to conclusions when confronting complexity. Valuing diversity can also help firms recruit and retain top talent.

Talent Analysis

Is our recruitment appropriate for our cultural and performance goals? Recruiters watch for a fit between an applicant and an organization's culture. The cost of a poor hire is high. However, insisting on always hiring the "the same kind of person" over and over is also dangerous and can result in "group think."

Is the orientation and onboarding process effective? Because first impressions count, and the first few days can set a lasting tone for a new hire, these processes must be carefully designed. It introduces the culture, demonstrates respect, and establishes expectations.

Do we have the skills we need for short- and long-term success? The success or failure of a company depends on employee skills and efforts. When employees have the opportunity to develop their skills, exercise autonomy, envisage their career, and participate in developmental assignments, their level of engagement and talent retention increases.

Are developmental opportunities comprehensive and effective? The way we do business is changing, so we must continually invest in our people. We require a systematic process to prepare a leadership pipeline for our future.

Do we retain our key talent? We must retain key talent by identifying what is key and who possesses those key skills. It can be difficult to obtain and costly to replace essential skills. Determining how to support and retain key talent gives us an extra edge in the marketplace.

Do people realize their full potential? Promotions, training, shadowing assignments, coaching, and on-the-job training produce a well-trained, highly skilled, and committed workforce.

Do leaders provide on-the-job developmental opportunities? Expertise develops from wide experience, effective training, and mentoring. To tap this expertise, we must implement succession planning, informal and formal development opportunities, and policies that support internal advancement.

Are employees effectively mentored or coached? Mentoring and coaching helps both parties gain insights into decision making, opportunities, and informal practices. Effective development goes beyond an infrequent performance review.

Is top management actively engaged in developing leaders of the future? Top managers are often the best trainers, coaches, and mentors available. Acting as a trainer or mentor is one way they can really leave a legacy. However, top-level managers must also polish their skills and continually develop.

Do we maintain our core competencies? Core competencies shift because of new strategies, new technologies, and new markets. Keeping competencies up-to-date prevents problems down the road.

Communication-Related

Do employees understand our traditions and goals? Employees have to understand the company's mission, market, strategy, and goals. Frequently, grand statements must be translated into more tangible language to guarantee a comprehensive understanding.

Is communication consistent with stated values, traditions, and goals? Goal confusion saps productivity. Communications should be consistent and align with strategy and actions. Unclear directives encourage mediocre performance because everyone waits to learn what is really wanted.

Policy Orientation

Are work practices fair and followed? When assignments, promotions, and recognition diverge from standards of fairness, employees adjust and start to "play the game"—an unproductive activity.

Is there an effective balance of work and life? Stress-induced burnout increases accidents, reduces decision quality, and increases turnover. And work-life balance is a high priority for the newest generations entering the workforce— along with a desire for fun.

Is recognition commensurate with performance? If poor and productive employees are treated equally, the message is that mediocre performance will be tolerated. What we recognize is what we will get.

Do our employees feel they have the autonomy needed to do their jobs? Micromanaging diminishes performance. A "wait for the boss to decide" mentality slows action and squashes initiative. Empowered workers contribute in terms of collaboration and creative thinking.

Is conflict managed promptly and effectively? Conflicts frequently deepen with time. Permitting personal, unit, or functional conflict to continue in the hope that things will resolve themselves won't work the vast majority of the time. Tackling issues early cuts distractions and returns attention to productive issues.

Are there clear resolution paths to handle questions or confusion? When new situations arise, they create questions and may stir tensions. Knowing how to promptly get answers and resolve confusion saves time and increases effectiveness.

SUMMARY AND NEXT STEPS

Only when you have, and retain, the best and brightest people do you have a continuing competitive advantage. Certainly as organizations reach maturity, they have a tendency to hold on to the formula that was instrumental to their success. But this is also a trap. Everything in the world moves, from the moon to events facing our organizations. Adjustments have to be continually introduced and carefully planned. Without our willingness to create a "best place to work" type of culture, no organization can become or remain world-class.

At some point, however, every organization confronts intense competition, shifting markets, and surprising twists and turns. Even dominant companies are challenged—Microsoft by Google, Nokia by Samsung. The rule of "creative destruction" operates in nature, life, and organizations. Therefore, we must constantly stay alert to trends, breakthroughs, and new ways of conducting business. Reading the signs enables us to be proactive.

It is so easy for us to become infatuated by the tried-and-true and to stick to what we have always done. This can cause us to ignore emerging trends and focus on the short-term. Yet, adjustments, shifts, and changes are frequently needed *before* the firestorm erupts.

Even stable, high-performing organizations with excellent cultures will ultimately have to reinvent themselves to survive in a turbulent and complex world. The Challenging Mindset, described in the next chapter, employs a future perspective to renew the organization and avoid destructive ruts.

Seizing Opportunities
The Challenging Mindset

————

It is important not that I be consistent with what I have said
but be consistent with the truth as it reveals itself to me.

—*Mahatma Gandhi*

Reasonable men adapt to their environment; unreasonable men try
to adapt the environment to themselves.

—*George Bernard Shaw*

The Challenging Mindset targets learning from current practices, discovering new ventures, and devising new business models to re-energize and sustain the organization. When we take the Challenging Mindset view of "pay me now or pay me later," we recognize that the cost of revitalization climbs higher the longer issues are not addressed. Therefore, we accept the need for rapid change and risk taking as an investment in future rewards. We view the pain or discomfort that accompanies strategic change as being a reasonable price to pay for new gains.

WHY LEADERS NEED THE CHALLENGING MINDSET

Organizations are ecosystems undergoing constant change rather than machines that perpetually perform as designed. When we adopt this mindset, we seek to prepare the organization for the future which understandably encounters resistance from those who cherish their current practices. (Sometimes, in fact, such resistance is warranted, as we'll later discuss.) Over the long run, however, undue resistance limits a company's future. Holding onto the status quo for too long frequently results in decline or dissolution by merger or, worse, bankruptcy. However, questioning the status quo or playing the devil's advocate is not easy or welcomed.

We naturally resist change that we have not introduced because ingrained habits are comfortable. However, routine creeps into and calcifies our thinking. Warren Buffet frequently reminds his audience of a Dr. Samuel Johnson quote: "The chains of habit are too light to be felt until they're too heavy to be broken."

Alert to the dangers of habit, we select the Challenging Mindset when we must champion new ideas and courageously prepare for the future. We recognize that even dominant companies falter. Only sixty-seven firms listed in the Fortune 500 companies in 1955 remained on the list in 2011. Four hundred and thirty-three firms were missing.

This churn among Fortune 500 firms should not surprise us. Changing demographics, economies, technologies, and competition are accelerating. In the past, we kept our landline equipment for decades, but now we are tempted to change our mobile phones every two years as new features are added and payment plans change. Startup companies pop up and then disappear in what seems like a blink of an eye. Sometimes they fold and sometimes are absorbed. Entrepreneurial startups typically last as long as the founder retains ownership—before the second generation takes charge. As the business life cycle quickens, our attention must frequently focus on renewal and revitalization, since the cost of ingrained and unexamined habits poses huge dangers.

A change-friendly and strategic orientation can be stymied at any stage. The *only* hope of avoiding a fixation on the past and a firm adherence to tradition is to draw on the Challenging Mindset. This strategic perspective with its future orientation cancels any tendency to rest on past laurels or to follow a stick-to-your-knitting philosophy.

FEATURES OF THE CHALLENGING MINDSET

Transitioning to the Challenging Mindset requires a willingness to question existing practices, operating assumptions, markets, and business models. We may shock those who just want to "get on with the business at hand" with these probes, but there are times when it is right to upset the apple cart to find better solutions. Confronting questions about new opportunities, brewing issues, and current assumptions may stir defensiveness or rejection. However, most of us like *progress* even as we dislike *change.* And, progress comes from change.

The difference is that progress offers us clear benefits, while change is an unknown quantity and therefore potentially dangerous. Everyone benefits with the early discovery of issues, opportunities, and problems, before damages register. Among the hallmarks of the Challenging Mindset are finding prospects to capture a windfall by being ahead the pack, preventing new competitors from entering into the market, and capturing unanticipated niches. Below are other hallmarks of this mindset in action.

View "Common Sense" as Malleable

Some concepts that appear to be no-brainers today were formerly considered radical. Walt Disney's request for a loan to fund a theme park was turned down by three hundred banks before he found one bank that could see the concept's promise. Today, funding would not be a problem. The Walt Disney Company controls media outlets including ABC and ESPN; studios including PIXAR, Disney, Touchstone, and Marvel; parks and resorts around the world; and a cruise line. Their success illustrates that it can be wise to ignore old standards about risk, old mantras about how organizations grow and thrive, and old assumptions about market competition.

History is filled with business leaders who ignored naysayers. David Sarnoff, head of RCA during the Depression, pushed television as he imagined it: a fully electronic system of scanning, broadcasting, and receiving moving images. He kept the faith despite a 1939 *New York Times* article on the debut of TV at the New York World's Fair saying "the problem with television is that the people must sit and keep their eyes glued on a screen; the average American family hasn't time for it." The 1946 RCA Victor television effectively slammed that assumption as bogus. For better or for worse, we are willing to watch screens of all types hour after hour.

Beware Ingrained Habits of Thought

Ken Olson, founder of Digital Equipment Corporation (DEC), asserted in 1977 that "there is no reason for anyone to have a computer in their home." His conclusion stemmed from DEC's market dominance in selling mini-computers, which he expected to endure. This assumption initially blinded him to opportunities of the personal computer. Even those who did see the home computer market erred in forecasting the speed of acceptance.

DEC is not alone in missing technology changes despite initial technology leadership. Microsoft captured the software market based on an alliance with IBM. With IBM focused on hardware, Microsoft had free rein in software and their market share swelled. With the 20/20 vision of hindsight, IBM might have made a different decision. While Microsoft's success intensified, it assumed that its software would always be dominant. Executives were late to recognize trends in mobile music, tablets, and smartphones—an error they are now addressing. Being an industry leader can generate blinders keeping us tied to outdated habits based on the premise that what worked in the past will continue to succeed in the future, despite evidence to the contrary.

Be Willing to Reinvent

History is filled with companies that successfully reinvented themselves proactively or reactively. Consider the example of the March of Dimes. President Franklin Roosevelt created the organization to combat polio. When the Salk vaccine was discovered in 1958, the March of Dimes could have declared victory and disbanded. However, it chose a new mission of fighting birth defects. Under such a large umbrella, their work continues.

General Electric is another firm that has experienced several reinventions. Jack Welch, a former CEO, sought new business possibilities in the 1980s. He required GE businesses to achieve or maintain first or second places in their markets or they would be sold. Though many thought it was reckless to shed profitable endeavors, he persisted jettisoning the high-visibility housewares business. Determined to lead the digitalization of the company, he sent roving "computer fanatics" on a mission to "destroy this business" and thereby reinvent the way business is done. Welch reframed the standard by relying on growth goals, rather than market position. In 2014, under CEO Jeff Immelt, GE planned to sell their appliance businesses and spin off their financial arm, cornerstones of the company's identity.

Organizations must adapt. Nokia began selling rubber boots before turning to electronics and cell phones. In 2014, it sold their cell phone business to Microsoft. And Royal Dutch Shell used to import and sell decorative shells before turning to oil. Subsequently it moved into biofuels and renewable energy. Nintendo sold playing cards until it moved into gaming by launching Donkey Kong. Video gaming consoles quickly followed. Reinvention is critical in our fast-paced world.

Look for New Options and Opportunities

Consider the traditional bookstore, a brick-and-mortar location where customers can inspect books, peruse a chapter, and discuss the book with staff. Established booksellers and publishers were confident in their ability to retain their business model. They underestimated the impact of technology. Amazon

CEO Jeff Bezos saw an alternative model. At first, much of the business community dismissed it as an inconsequential fad.

Convinced that readers insisted on touching and reviewing a hard copy, traditional booksellers did little at first to prevent losses to an untested cyber entity. Amazon overcame the disadvantages of its virtual nature by offering reader reviews, author interviews, "one-click" shopping, and discount pricing. While not providing a place for people to congregate, the site offered an alternative electronic community and a huge catalog.

Bezos's nontraditional strategy stemmed from nontraditional thinking. During hiring interviews, he asked oddball questions to assess potential executive candidates' thinking skills. One of his questions—How many gas stations are there in the United States?—was not intended to elicit a precise count. Its purpose was to allow Bezos to assess the mental dexterity of the applicant. His own response developed from his knowledge that his own small hometown in Texas had three thousand people and two gas stations. Multiplying that number by the total U.S. population, he arrived at a figure of 175,000 stations—just 6.7 percent shy of the 186,600 total given by the American Petroleum Institute at the time. He also sought to test creative problem solving by asking executive candidates to tell him of an instance when the candidate identified and solved a problem that everyone thought was unsolvable.

Discount pricing is now common throughout the industry, most major bookstore chains have an online presence, and distribution channels have consolidated. Business assumptions were smashed once new models succeeded.

Amazon's scope also shifted. It began offering fulfillment services to other firms, and it expanded product lines to sell used books, products from other retailers, and offerings from high-end retailers such as Neiman Marcus.

The introduction of iTunes, online weight programs, and online college courses demonstrates how the digital revolution continues to disrupt traditional business models. It is hazardous to underestimate how technology changes barriers to entry, customer expectations, brand status, and cost models. Technology obsolescence is a major risk confronting a wide array of businesses. Even shopping malls must adjust to online shopping trends.

Question Old Assumptions

Medtronic patented the first internal pacemaker and then expanded into heart defibrillators as well as other devices. But it also rethought assumptions about what types of facilities should provide defibrillators. Instead of restricting them to hospitals and ambulances, Medtronic encouraged making them accessible in gyms, offices, and airports. Because the first fifteen minutes after a heart attack is critical, Medtronic repositioned the medical device as comparable to fire extinguishers and argued it should, therefore, be as available at work and at home.

By rethinking assumptions, companies discover new markets, as Medtronic has, but also invent new business models. Following are several examples:

- Airbnb rethought accommodations by creating a brokerage service that offered homeowners the opportunity to rent rooms in their residences.
- The company NetJets gave customers a new choice besides either buying a plane or flying commercial. Capitalizing on pent-up demand for point-to-point flights, NetJets sells fractions of specific aircraft to "owners."
- The company Curves for Women created a gym with machinery and routines specifically designed for women.
- Keurig opened new markets with the K-Cup for coffee and expanded it to other drinks. And Green Mountain Coffee partnered with Coca-Cola to develop single pod servings of cold Coke.
- Uber disrupted the taxi industry by shifting the concept of cab service, thereby cutting investment costs and eliminating the need for a dispatcher.

React to Trends

Although disruption happens in all fields, some industries experience periods of intense flux. The U.S. healthcare industry has been upended by the passage of the Affordable Care Act (ACA), demographic shifts, new medical practices, new and public rankings, and technological advances. In this environment, healthcare companies must respond effectively, demonstrating a willingness to abandon prized practices, form new alliances, and impose new standards to handle new expectations.

Ferrokin BioSciences shook pharmaceutical industry practices by using virtual contractors rather than by employing scientists to develop new therapies. In addition, it shortened the regulatory approval process by streamlining the connection between doctors and regulators. This new relationship put products on shelves much faster. The firm was purchased by a Dublin pharmaceutical in 2012, partially due to its ability to obtain fast FDA approval. The use of virtual healthcare organizations continues to grow, as does the use of free agents.

Adopting the Challenging Mindset also means being willing to eliminate products or practices that are falling out of favor. Canceling existing products may be necessary. Products that have been pulled from the market include everything from Regular Coca-Cola with Lime to the incandescent light bulb. Shinola, which was founded in 1907, produced wax shoe polish until 1960. It now manufactures bicycles and watches. This radical shift was caused by changes in demand, material costs, and replacement products. Organizations must stay alert to early market signs and keep pace with the market to remain viable.

Berkshire Hathaway turned away from textiles because of foreign competition. It became an investment powerhouse under Warren Buffet. Wipro, currently one of India's largest IT service firms, started by selling vegetables and home goods. It has since seized new opportunities in outsourcing IT services to become the "IBM of India."

Rethink Relationships

Sidney Harman, founder of high-fidelity component manufacturer Harman International Industries, advocated the idea of challenging orthodoxy. One way he did this was to refashion labor relations in his Bolivar, Tennessee, plant after hearing about conditions from one of the plant workers. The Bolivar Project encouraged worker engagement and served as a model for many subsequent management programs across the U.S. The move paid off when the union renewed a contract earlier than required, enabling the firm to win a key General Motors contract.

Former competitors can also become supporters. Microsoft and Apple competed over operating systems and even brought lawsuits against each other. Then a new relationship was forged and Microsoft invested in Apple. Competitor-to-partner shifts happen more often than expected. International airlines turned from direct competition into code-sharing operations. But not all relationships are between for-profit organizations.

For-profit firms also establish relationships with nonprofits. Macy's "Wear Red" campaign, for example, supported the American Heart Association. Avon supported breast cancer research and Whirlpool partners with Habitat for Humanity. Even cities that formerly vied for tourism in a region have found that combined campaigns provide a bigger boost.

Union leaders can also identify new and productive relationships. James Hunter, head of Local 1900 of the International Brotherhood of Electrical Workers (IBEW), operated within the standard adversarial framework in his dealings with the management of the Potomac Electric Power Company (Pepco). Having fought a 2004 merger between Pepco and another local electric company that eventually derailed, and facing contract negotiations that were expected to be contentious, Hunter wrote John Derrick, chairman of Pepco, and made an unusual offer—a one-year contract extension. Pepco accepted, and some traditional and nontraditional joint operations followed.

When the Maryland legislature considered a deregulation bill that the company considered unacceptable, Hunter and his IBEW members for the first time lobbied the legislature on behalf of the company. They set up phone banks and bused members to the capital with handmade signs to tell their legislators of their concerns about the bill. This cooperation halted consideration of the bill. Assumptions about what was possible had changed, but any shift of this magnitude cannot be considered permanent unless it is regularly reinforced.

Remember Nothing Is Permanent

Even successful reinventions will not remain that way indefinitely. Renewal and reinvention continues as new options or new demands surface. Take the example of Frances Hesselbein, who in 1976 assumed the position as executive director of the Girl Scouts of the U.S.A., an organization with 750,000 adult leaders and more than 2.4 million active members. Against a backdrop of falling membership and programs in need of rejuvenation, Hesselbein committed to building a pluralistic organization that would serve young girls, from the inner city to the countryside. With a new image, new approaches, and new energy, Girl Scouts membership grew.

But like all successful reinventions, the Girl Scouts' reinvention became ingrained and it eventually fell out of touch with new realities. In 2013, membership had fallen, volunteer leadership had declined, and pension costs had led to the sale of camps. The severity of the challenges resulted in substantial reductions in regional councils. Today, a new debate about the organization's culture and future has emerged.

Another example comes from the National Geographic Society, which produces *National Geographic* magazine. Its success in photo journalism is unquestioned, but its audience was shifting to other media. And so did National Geographic. It harnessed social media and established a cable TV channel to reinvent its brand and expand into the travel industry.

Reinvention has also continued for American Express, which started as the Pony Express. After giving up on horse transcontinental communication, it started providing traveler's checks and other services to vacationers. Recognizing the limited market size, it expanded into offering revolving credit cards for the consumer market and small businesses.

Be Bold (But Smart About It)

Taking on a government-supported agency may seem like a quixotic endeavor, but Tony DeSio did just that. He boldly created a franchise model firm to compete with United States Postal Services (USPS). He leveraged an agreement with UPS and convinced franchisees to allocate a portion of income for national advertising. This ultimately changed minds and practices. Mail Boxes Etc. grew into four thousand outlets by the time DeSio retired in 1997. In 2001, the chain was purchased by the United Parcel Service, which renamed the chain The UPS Store.

John Hendricks, who created Discovery Communications in the mid-1970s, was also bold and smart in exploiting a niche overlooked by the big networks. Nature programming was not considered interesting or engaging enough to attract sizable audiences. Hendricks thought otherwise. He expanded globally, relying on local talent to select content for each locale. While CBS, NBC, and ABC were busy monitoring each other as the major threats to their future, cable TV grew into a hard-to-ignore competitor. Discovery acquired The Learning Channel as well as travel, health, and other properties. Today it operates in 39 languages and offers both non-fiction and fiction programming to 1.5 billion subscribers.

Adapt to New Technologies and Interests

Reuters International has provided financial news for more than 150 years through a subscriber model. They provide access to real-time quotes, data on futures contracts, and other financial information through their proprietary technology. When the World Wide Web arrived, Tom Glocer, the first non-journalist CEO of Reuters, boosted digital access by providing services across a variety of platforms. By shifting its technologies, he positioned the firm for an eventual acquisition by Thompson in 2008. The firm has expanded from a financial operational into legal summaries for attorneys.

The increasing reliance on mobile technology has shifted not only marketing strategies but also manufacturing and retailing operations. Generational change also requires adjustments. By leveraging technology, Twitter, Snapchat, Pinterest, Instagram, and universal translations services offer new services that were unheard of a few years ago. New is here to stay until it is surpassed by something "newer."

Other Features

In addition to the features discussed above, leaders operating from the Challenging Mindset generally concentrate on the following:

- Stress the need to keep an eye on the big picture
- Scan for trends
- Recognize issue s and limitations associated with the current business model
- Encourage reasonable risk taking
- Accept paradox and ambiguity
- Champion substantive change when warranted
- Value diverse perspectives and cross-discipline thinking
- Examine sacred cows and outdated practices
- Promote flexibility for sustained success
- Encourage multiple viewpoints to discover optimal solutions
- Convince others of the need for agility and change readiness
- Learn from experiences and apply those lessons across the organization
- Identify potential partners, alliances, or acquisitions

SELECTING THE CHALLENGING MINDSET AS A PRIORITY

When is it time for us to deploy a Challenging Mindset? Obviously, we must do it when technology takes a leap forward, but we also must adopt this mindset when our business models veer from market realities. Other instances include when:

- Our industry is shaken by new competitors
- Global markets undercut our brands
- Thinking has stagnated to the point that every new opportunity is being rejected as too risky

- We are holding onto past practices and policies
- There is an intense fear that change will "cannibalize" existing product lines
- The same errors in judgment are repeated

These situations require a trailblazing approach combined with systematic analysis to identify what products or business lines must be abandoned to secure the future. This mindset examines whether our viewpoints are clouded, whether habit has replaced the need to reexamine opportunities, and whether it is time to ensure that we elicit dissenting points of view.

If our organization seeks renewal, revitalization, or rejuvenation, the Challenging Mindset should take center stage. If the organization is losing ground to hungrier, more innovative competitors, this mindset is critical to investigate the need for change, pursue new ventures and alliances, and support innovative thinking. It rekindles the appetite for greater agility and enhanced initiative.

AVOIDING IMBALANCES

Electing this, or any, priority does not relieve us of the need to constantly monitor our situation. Recent customer feedback, changes in quality, new regulations, or disruptions in the supply chain can pop up at any time and may take precedence. Agility, not consistency, is crucial.

Although we select the Challenging Mindset when our organization is in need of strategic change, we must still remain alert to key internal issues. We cannot allow ourselves to become so dazzled by our grand strategic initiative that we become blinded to more mundane concerns.

We must also balance our feelings of confidence and enthusiasm with a recognition that strategic planning and forecasting are still more an art than a science. A Challenging Mindset must retain a sense of humility. After all, history has shown that prognostications tend to be notoriously inaccurate on everything from the stock market to the weather. Even Albert Einstein erred when he stated in 1932 that "there is not the slightest indication that [nuclear energy] will ever be obtainable. It would mean that the atom would have to be shattered at will."

Maintaining balance means being both dynamic and prudent—not an easy combination. To use a baseball metaphor, some with this mindset might swing at every pitch, aiming for the home run, while others recognize that a single forcing in a run might be more sensible.

The Challenging Mindset's desire to see around corners into the future may result in detecting shadows rather than real trends or opportunities. Given that it embraces new ideas, there is the danger that some alternatives may be discounted at the cost of morale, talent retention or productivity. Catching the next wave can produce rewards, but will it provide a lasting payoff? Then there is the potential that another promising venture will pop up and divert the Challenging Mindset from its current focus. Those who prioritize this mindset should be wary of jumping from idea to idea without fully committing to a single venture.

Despite promise or hoopla, the Challenging Mindset cannot automatically turn promise into reality. Successful execution comes only after the enactment of realistic projections, detailed plans, earned support, and effective execution processes. To attain success, infrastructure, quality, customers, culture, and innovation must all contribute.

Balance Optimism with Realism

Imbalances in the Challenging Mindset emerge when ventures far afield from core competencies are undertaken, when resources are overextended, and when scant thought is given to gaining active support. This mindset recognizes when change is needed, but it may not correctly assess what is feasible, reasonable, or doable. It may also rely on technological solutions that are implausible or untested. Pronouncing that a new business model is wise cannot be confused with a *fait accompli.* The current status or equilibrium resists what might be considered a wild swing or temporary fancy. Support cannot be assumed; it has to be earned.

Strategic repositioning initiatives have low success rates. They fail seventy percent of the time. When we operate from the Challenging Mindset we fall prey to the "proclaim it and they will come" fallacy. But that is not the only problem. An imbalanced Challenging Mindset can conjure wacky plans, including quirky acquisitions that are later divested at a substantial loss.

Iridium LLC, for example, spent $150 million on advertising and five billion dollars putting satellites into orbit in the hope that its sixty-six satellite system would support worldwide telecommunications. Although the market appeared broad, it was quite narrow. Subscribers were those in mid-ocean, at the poles, or in other isolated areas beyond the reach of cell towers. Confronted with a nimble cell phone industry and falling equipment prices, Iridium found it difficult to establish the anticipated beachhead. After introducing a bulky and expensive phone that would not work indoors, Iridium went bankrupt in 1999. However, in 2001, private investors purchased Iridium's assets for $25 million and repositioned the company to focus on government contracts. In 2009, Iridium Communications was listed on the NASDAQ exchange, serving an essential function for remote scientific and government locations.

Another example of overconfidence can be seen in Aetna, Inc. The 148-year-old Hartford-based firm, suffered from a mismatch between aspiration and reality. In 1998, Aetna went on a buying spree, purchasing U.S. Healthcare, NYL Care, and Prudential Insurance's healthcare business. Some questioned the price paid for the firms, while others questioned Aetna's ability to implement its strategy successfully. Within a few years, then CEO John Rowe (2000-2006) said, "We bit off more than we could chew."

Challenging Mindsets may see the allure of the possible but underestimate the constraints in determining what is probable. Plans can be captured on paper, but that does not make them real. Results, not plans, are what count.

Below are additional indicators that the Challenging Mindset has become unbalanced:

There is a high level of churn

1. New programs or initiatives are regularly introduced and cast aside.
2. Management fads are introduced without appropriate customization or tailoring to the organization.
3. Frequent changes create confusion and/or sap commitment.

There is a lack of alignment

4. Operational plans and goals are not driven by strategic plans.
5. More effort is allocated to strategic planning than execution planning.
6. Systems are not realigned to support new strategic directions.
7. Differences of opinion surface on whether the firm is heading in the right direction.
8. Strategic planning is disconnected from those who will execute the plan.
9. Change violates core identity or values.
10. Insufficient resources, including time, are allocated to achieve the strategic plan.

There are communication problems

11. Communication concentrates on actions rather than on explaining context and anticipated benefits.
12. Input from current customers is missing or ignored.
13. Limited information is available on how the plans impact units.
14. Few measures or detailed plans are developed for the early execution stage.
15. Rosy forecasts present an idyllic and assured outcome.

There are cultural barriers to success

16. No one steps up to serve as a committed sponsor or champion.
17. People are pushed to "get on board" and labeled "resisters" for asking questions or expressing concerns.
18. A "go it alone" approach overlooks potential alliances and partnerships.
19. Time pressure is used to reject calls for modifications or adjustments.

ASSESSING CURRENT CONDITIONS

The Challenging Mindset welcomes rapid and substantial change to cope with rapidly changing circumstances. It is comfortable with ambiguity, paradoxes, and complexity. This mindset stresses a strategic perspective rather than short-term wins.

Criteria that drive the Challenging Mindset include growth trajectories of current products, economic or demographic trends, new technologies, and business trends that present new opportunities.

In addition, leaders should assess the organizational life cycle, organizational culture, and market realities to determine if this mindset becomes a priority. The following questions can help with this assessment:

Opportunity Questions

- What opportunities exist at this time?
- How can we leverage our strengths?
- What new business model could be employed?
- What strategic alliances or acquisitions would position us for the future?
- How can we increase our agility and change readiness?
- How can technology or other advances contribute to our future?
- What emerging customer expectations and trends can we leverage?

Risk Questions

- What nontraditional threats could surface?
- How do internal gaps, shortcomings or issues limit our success?
- What significant trends or patterns are affecting us or will affect us in the near future?
- Are there signs that the market for our products and services are on the verge of stagnating or even declining?

Cultural Questions

- Are we resting on our laurels?
- Is there evidence of "groupthink"?
- What assumptions may no longer be valid?
- Are we effectively learning from internal and external experience?

Strategy Questions

- What would we be doing differently if we were starting our business today?
- What broader goals are possible?
- How can we encourage strategic thinking and planning at all levels?

By offering a flexible response to new business circumstances, the Challenging Mindset willingly exchanges risks for increased benefits. Reassessing plans or presenting an iconoclastic alternative can stir constructive tension, discussion, and discovery. When dissenting views are valued, the chance of misjudgment and overreach is minimized. While some may see different viewpoints as too stressful or unwieldy, the Challenging Mindset assumes that pressure produces diamonds. These tensions also protect against stagnation while serving to revitalize the organization.

SHARPENING THE CHALLENGING MINDSET

The Challenging Mindset's penchant for rejecting the status quo and detecting trends in search of vitality and sustainability undercuts stability. Recognizing the impact of the product life cycle, this mindset reformulates goals to harvest new opportunities. Like a chess master, the Challenging Mindset strategically plots moves and countermoves. At other times, unlike the chess master, the Challenging Mindset boldly sweeps away the rules of the game and lays out a newer version. Whether methodical or daring, this mindset stirs thinking, engages energies, and encourages a broad view of the future.

Unfettered by precedent, the Challenging Mindset reorients thinking by considering the new, promising, overlooked, or unfashionable alternative. For example, we may use this mindset to question traditional thinking that bigger firms are always better or that the first firm to bring a product to market always has an unbeatable advantage. Instead, many organizations find that smaller units tap entrepreneurial energy and effectiveness. And, firms that follow a market leader frequently flourish, including Amazon—which was the second firm to enter the online bookselling business.

Being able to rethink positions enables us to avoid perilous pitfalls and uncovers promising new alternatives. If prospects appear bleak, we may seek to change the rules or the game. Rather than extrapolate from the past, this lens seeks to forge a new and sustainable path.

If we want to prioritize the Challenging Mindset in our organization, we can jumpstart it with the following questions.

Monitoring the Business Environment

Are systems in place to examine practices and test assumptions? If they are not, it will be hard to identify the need for change in order to adapt to emerging trends.

Are we able to identify potential threats? Every organization needs an early alert system to foresee threats and avoid unpleasant surprises. An effective monitoring practice provides more time for proactive responses.

Are we monitoring nontraditional as well as traditional threats? Monitoring systems must be able to detect unconventional as well as conventional risks. After all, truly paradigm-changing threats often come from new and unexpected competitors.

Can we identify and seize opportunities? Translating trends and threats into opportunities boosts sustainability. Taking the leap forward is daunting but frequently essential. The organization should constantly be on the outlook for new opportunities.

Are environmental trends understood? Knowing the trends is only part of the challenge confronting decision makers. Understanding them and their implications requires careful analysis of actual risks and opportunities.

Organizational Adaptability

Are we a trendsetter in our industry? Organizations with this distinction typically operate from a future focus characteristic of the Challenging Mindset, but so do other firms that adopt a fast follower strategy.

Are we revising our policies and systems to meet emerging needs? Systems must be reconfigured to increase adaptability. Current systems may be rewarding behavior that is no longer critical.

Are effective best practices being institutionalized? Discovering internal best practices that fit your needs and unique corporate culture are rarely shared or adopted. Organizations must provide active support if they want internal best practices to become widespread.

Are critical thinking and change management rewarded? If not, we are more likely to resist ideas or proposals that alter the status quo.

Is it safe to be a "devil's advocate"? If questioning an idea results in shunning or discounting the person with a different view, the message becomes "play it safe and close to the vest."

What will make us more agile and responsive to change? Asking questions, encouraging initiative, rewarding change agents, and encouraging comprehensive analysis build a change-ready culture.

Do we systematically learn from our experience? Learning from experience and mistakes enables us to avoid repeating them in the future. Instead of viewing a systematic review as a search to affix blame, it must be equated with a desire to continually improve.

Are we improving our planning process? Planning is not just an annual event by top executives. Planning integration, monitoring, and modification at all levels is key.

Is conformity, or "groupthink," sidetracking our long-term success? The decision-making process that starts with the leader announcing a decision encourages groupthink. An organizational leader will get better ideas if we promote the expression of challenging new thoughts, recognize dissenting points of view, and listen to all viewpoints.

Are we building for our future? This question jolts thinking and opens the door to a wide range of ideas and opportunities. Most of us enjoy defining our desired future state.

Strategic Thinking

Are we effectively leveraging technology? We often underutilize our systems capabilities or reject the need for new systems. This can endanger customer retention, integration, and outcomes.

Are we addressing emerging customer expectations and trends? As product life cycles shorten, we must move quickly. Otherwise, we will lose our customers that we worked hard to attract in the first place.

Are we effectively balancing long- and short-term goals? When we focus only on the short-term, we run a high risk of being blind-sided by emerging trends. If we only focus on the long-term, we may not survive long enough to reap long-term benefits.

Have we identified strategic alliances or partnerships? Alliances provide access to scarce talent, greater capacity, larger markets or additional resources to position us for the future.

Is critical thinking rewarded by both recognition and career advancement? Traditionally we reward those who fight fires or solve a current problem. However, we must balance this recognition by acknowledging those who demonstrate a strategic perspective and support new endeavors.

[169]

Is strategic thinking used every day? Strategic thinking cannot become tied to a retreat or a brainstorming session. It must be applied to even innocuous decisions to guarantee that risks have been fully assessed, feasibility fully tested, and integration leveraged.

SUMMARY AND NEXT STEPS

Whether or not we adopt the Challenging Mindset as our current priority, the perspective remains a key aspect in our thinking. We must cultivate it to prevent conventional thinking from squashing new alliances, plans or ventures. To effectively position ourselves for the future, we must operate based on a comprehensive understanding of the evolving context and a willingness to investigate new opportunities.

Since the future is where we all are going, we need fresh thinking and new perspectives so that we arrive prepared as we progress toward our desired destination. We must be willing and able to identify and implement timely mid-course adjustments that sidestep the need for drastic infusion of new resources or the uncomfortable choice of abandoning an initiative.

We can use this mindset to provide us with a blueprint for pursuing new ventures, product lines, or market segments. As insights are gained, attention transitions from the Challenging Mindset where novel concepts are considered to the Inventing Mindset where ideas translate into tangible new offerings.

Mindset balance requires constant monitoring. The need for innovation and risk has to be balanced with the desire for smooth operations. And the need to prepare for the future must be offset by the desire for clear structure and systems. Juggling demands and opportunities to ensure that organization thrives and endures requires wise decisions and implementation.

Recognizing and weighing all the mindsets ensures an agile, practical, and united response to uncertainty and complexity. There is a spectrum of factors that can blindside us if we neglect to use all six mindset lenses. Like the kaleidoscope where one small adjustment significantly alters entire pictures, one change sends out reverberations across the organization. The mindset framework insures that these impacts are identified and evaluated to capture benefits and minimize risks. Using mindsets facilitates understanding of the context bolstering support for action. It also builds a change-ready culture.

The next chapters describe how these mindsets can gain support for change, defuse conflict, and foster alignment.

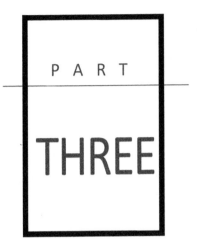

PART

THREE

Leveraging the Power
of Mindsets

———

9

Deploying Mindsets to Impact Conflict and Influence

The only way on earth to influence the other fellow is to talk about what he wants and show him how to get it.

—*Dale Carnegie*

If there is any one secret of success, it lies in the ability to get the other person's point of view and see things from his angle as well as from your own.

—Henry Ford

If you would persuade, you must appeal to interest rather than intellect.

—Benjamin Franklin

Using mindsets, we can effectively defuse unproductive conflict by discovering better solutions and actions. We can also facilitate communication and boost our influence when we understand how mindsets shape thinking. Since our perception is our reality, expanding our ability to see different viewpoints changes our view of what is possible and what builds bridges. It also increases our respect for different perspectives and encourages us to carefully listen to others. Truth is more frequently discovered when we listen more than we speak. The mindset framework provides a template for how to listen, lead, influence, and coach effectively. Consider implementing the following actions:

1. Identify your current mindset and probe for other perspectives. Greater exploration produces better decisions while also framing the issue as an objective examination rather than a personal agenda or pre-ordained decision.
2. Collect information in all six mindset areas for analysis to reduce risk and unwelcomed surprises. This also removes potential blinders before they distort your decision-making process. You can also move beyond "easy answers" to develop brilliant plans.
3. Groom new talent by showing them how to weigh multiple factors and assess the full scope of context.
4. Encourage respect for different viewpoints to improve teaming and collaboration. The team can also use the mindset questions in the next chapter to measure how to validate their thinking and analysis.
5. Craft communication to provide context and define expected benefits. Detect the driving mindset to craft effective messages and interpret questions and concerns. Validating and discussing another's perspective increases our influence. In an age when we frequently work with new people, you have to understand what drives others. After all, if we do not have followers, how can we be leaders?

CONFLICT AND CLASHES

Conflict consumes thirty percent of our time in organizations, no matter what the level. From the C-suite to the factory floor, a wide assortment of concerns, rumors, fears, and slights spring to life. When these go unresolved they escalate, producing hardened interpersonal conflict. One reason tension goes unresolved is that many of us hold out a persistent hope that things will magically resolve themselves without intervention. Unfortunately, many disputes do not. They simmer and then erupt into disruptive conflict where it is difficult to achieve a full resolution.

Tension typically starts when another's behavior or action registers as inappropriate or mistaken. With time, the deviation appears more significant. In fact, this stage can be called the "difference of opinion" stage. The observer assumes that the colleague operates from a different set of goals and misunderstands what is expected of him or her.

As time passes, the idiosyncratic behavior advances from a minor blip to a key annoyance and finally it develops into a personal clash. This escalation produces withdrawal, avoidance or rejection. If these growing tensions are ignored, the conflict shifts again into resistance, complaints and negative stereotypes. Without resolution, scorn for another's personal standards, ethics, values, and principles deepen, transforming discomfort and displeasure into open conflict and hardened judgments. Unwinding this antagonistic level is thorny. Formal requests to shake hands and put differences aside rarely work. Uneasiness remains despite requests to start fresh. A residue lingers.

The best time to resolve conflicts is during the early "difference of opinion" stage, before attitudes freeze and judgments form. At this early stage, there is the real possibility of exploring viewpoints, unearthing synergies, and finding common ground. In fact, the difference may be highly constructive in discovering unconventional ideas or testing different approaches. Unfortunately, many of us fail to effectively handle this stage, hoping for a self-generated, mutually satisfactory resolution so the issue will become old news and evaporate.

However, optimistic thinking is frequently misplaced and is followed by an antagonistic stage where trust and respect suffer and patience dissolves. Each party sees the other as "different" and less worthy, so cooperation breaks down, accusations fly either publicly or through the grapevine, and productivity suffers. At this stage, each party wants to "win" the conflict by proving the other person wrong. Dysfunction is obvious and there is limited likelihood that a lasting fix can be found.

How to Use the Mindset Approach

A more effective strategy in resolving emerging quarrels is to view differences as disparate mindsets. If we can view another person's conclusions as stemming from a different but valid mindset, then we can reduce the odds that our differences of opinion will blossom into a full-fledged personal conflict. When we recognize that another's perspective has merit, we stop judging and shift our thinking. We swerve from discounting or demonizing the other party into synthesizing and aligning mindsets.

The Leadership Spectrum Wheel, which we saw earlier in Chapter 2, illustrates the sequence in which different mindsets progress and also helps us understand potential conflict points.

Figure Three: The Leadership Spectrum Wheel

When mindsets are opposite each other on the Wheel, conscious or subconscious tension based on contrasting goals and focal points is likely. The mindsets that are most likely to diverge are:

Inventing and Performing
Catalyzing and Protecting
Challenging and Developing

These difference stem from three sources: (1) focusing primarily on *external* or *internal* environmental issues, (2) encouraging *fast* change or *incremental* change and (3) electing to *accept risk* or *reduce risk* for the future. In essence, the mindsets associated with Inventing, Catalyzing, and Challenging stress external factors, prefer fast change, and equate reasonable risk taking with opportunity. In contrast, those operating from the Developing, Performing, and Protecting mindsets target internal issues, prefer incremental change, and seek to mitigate risk as the best way to serve the organization and meet current challenges.

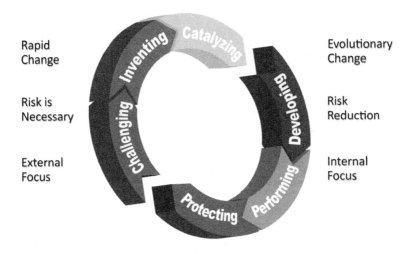

Rapid
Change

Risk is
Necessary

External
Focus

Evolutionary
Change

Risk
Reduction

Internal
Focus

Figure Four: Hemisphere Orientations

When mindsets clash, it does not have to escalate into open conflict. Asking the team to explore all viewpoints reveals how each contributes and calms tension. By surfacing facts, research, experience, and assumptions, we are able to find common ground before differences burst into dysfunctional conflict.

Consider the situation where a new externally hired CEO joined an established, fast-growing firm. His marching orders from his board were to continue on a path of fast growth (the Catalyzing Mindset) so he took the helm convinced that the strategic goal was continued expansion. His executive team resisted, arguing that the organization needed to focus on developing a succession plan (the Protecting Mindset) and increasing quality (the Performing Mindset). At first the CEO attributed the reluctance to displeasure with his appointment, since two members of his team had applied for his position. Luckily, his opinion changed. He objectively listened to his staff's thoughts without ascribing labels or hidden agendas.

He discovered that the firm's most valued customers were complaining about quality problems and poor customer service. Complaints mounted and some customers remarked that contracts might not be renewed unless things changed. As a result, the CEO redirected efforts to save existing customers through quality improvement before tackling the mandate to grow. He acknowledged that if quality concerns went public, opportunities for expansion would ultimately fail. He elected to tackle the quality issues first. In this case, the CEO avoided prolonged conflict by incorporating legitimate concerns into a goal that the whole team supported.

This was a healthy outcome which demonstrates the value of tapping into all the team's knowledge prior to setting goals. By viewing the corporate landscape from the vantage of mindsets, we make wiser decision and gain active support for implementation. We must restrain our desire to convince others of our viewpoint until we learn how others assess the situation.

Seek First to Understand

In the U.S., there is an assumption that conversation is a competitive sport and the first person who stops to take a breath loses. Talking rather than listening is preferred, since listening appears passive and is falsely assumed to be a waste of time. Too often, we see our role as speaking, espousing, inspiring and promoting ideas rather than listening to others. In fact, the opposite is true. Listening provides information, enabling leaders to detect the topics that are likely to persuade. We gain quite a bit more information from listening, asking questions, and determining the other person's mindset than we do by trying to sell our own.

The Catholic prayer seeking "to be understood as to understand" was renewed in Stephen Covey's *Seven Habits of Highly Effective People* as "seeking first to understand" before being understood. Great advice. The only question is how do we understand another's viewpoint? How can we correctly interpret another's driving mindset?

The historical phrase "a penny for your thoughts" illustrates how easy it is to find out what another person is thinking. Just ask. Barbara Walters, an interview expert, suggested in her book, *How to Talk With Practically Anybody About Practically Anything*, that all you have to do is make an inquiry such as, "Tell me about yourself" and the other person will "talk for hours."

In short, questions elicit a wealth of knowledge as long as we have a framework to analyze what we hear. Asking the other person is tapping the ultimate resource. Of course, the question varies. Some options include:

- What goals are you working on right now?
- What are critical issues or challenges in your view?
- What would you like to see happen next?
- What opportunities do you want to capture?
- What keeps you awake at night?

Responses to these questions reveal a person's mindset. No super sleuthing or psychoanalysis is required. By listening, we can determine the current mindset and start to explore mutually satisfactory outcomes. We can also jointly identify areas for further examination.

For example, if a colleague's focus is on product quality or customer return, then we can assume that she is prioritizing the Performing Mindset. On the other hand, if she is more focused on the future and new alliances, she is much more likely to emphasize the Challenging Mindset. The first, the Performing Mindset, wants to fine-tune existing processes while the Challenging Mindset seeks to explore new horizons. Depending on which priority is operating, we would adjust our approach, since one has a risk reduction goal while the other invites reasonable risk taking.

Of course, we do prioritize more than one mindset at a time, but we are highly unlikely to prioritize all six. Our research indicates that forty-five percent of the leaders surveyed currently focused on one mindset. What's more, fully ninety-eight percent of six thousand respondents in our research operate from three or fewer mindsets. Therefore, we can hone in on the one or two current mindsets by asking questions and deciphering responses.

Use the Profile Predictor to Gain Insights

Certainly there are occasions when a direct inquiry is not feasible, and in these instances we can consider what we have heard, witnessed, or know about current plans and action. In these instances, the Priority Predictor Chart (see Table Three below) provides insights. If we review the "Considers Valuable" column, we look at matching actions or desired outcomes to a mindset or priority. We have a preliminary indicator of their current mindset.

In some cases, *dislikes* are more clearly known than *likes*. In these instances, review the "Considers Undesirable" column to gain an initial mindset indicator. Findings from both the "Valuable" and "Undesirable" columns guide us in kicking off a conversation which will confirm or correct our assumption.

Starting a conversation from another's viewpoint increases the probability that constructive dialogue will follow. Remember it is wise, even if it is difficult, to put your thoughts and goals second and emphasize listening at the outset. This keeps your mind open to new perspectives and gives you the opportunity to think before you speak – always a smart option. In addition, you can notice commonalities that become a solid foundation for discussion instead of heated debate.

Table Three: Priority Predictor Chart

PRIORITY PREDICTOR		
Mindset	**Considers Valuable**	**Considers Undesirable**
Inventing	Exploration of new options Discretionary time to pursue ideas Systems that reward innovation Challenging tasks	Excessive structure Tight deadlines Routine assignments Short-term thinking Resistance to new ideas
Catalyzing	"Can do" orientation Flexibility Personal communication Clear goals Customer focus	Slow decision making Process details Fear of rapid growth Lack of commitment Lost time, delay
Developing	Objective organizational analysis Systems perspective Macro viewpoint Delegation Structure and planning	Confusion or chaos Tangential thinking Ineffective systems Inadequate operational analysis Lack of clear responsibility
Performing	Analytical orientation Reliance on data and results Incremental improvements Direct communication Expertise/knowledge	Missing or withheld information Subjectivity Turf mentality or sub-optimization Performance gaps Inattention to the "bottom line"
Protecting	Preparedness Cautious decision making Tradition and loyalty Personnel development Sense of identity and community	Change for the sake of change Unwarranted risk Conflict Failure to consider procedures Short-term orientation
Challenging	Future orientation Reflection and learning Ambiguity Change Questioning of assumptions	Missed opportunities Resistance to new perspectives Lack of strategic focus Reliance on the status quo Ignoring trends

Source: Leadership Spectrum Profile®. © Enterprise Management Ltd.,
1998–2012.

Build Common Bonds When Possible

Common connections and mindsets foster respect and comfort. We quickly link with others when we find almost any similarity: athletes playing together on the same team, tourists finding another person from their city in a foreign location, people driving the same model car, conference attendees presenting to their peers, high-school alumni gathering together, or strangers coping with shared experiences such as a hurricane or blizzard.

In social situations we also search for ways to connect. Our introductions identify potential bonds and we listen for commonalities in another's background, interest areas or thinking to anchor a connection. While diversity helps us avoid blunders, commonalities build relationships, trust, and engagement. Whether superficial or substantial, these ties trigger perceptions of mutuality and facilitate constructive exchanges.

Common connections build mutual respect and increase prospects for partnering and collaboration. When commonality is perceived, respect is gained and the prospect is that the parties will partner and collaborate. Without a common connection and an uncertain level of respect, interaction vacillates between ignoring and resisting the other person as depicted in Table Four.

Table Four: Levels of Perceived Commonality

	High Respect or Comfort	Undetermined Respect or Comfort
High Commonality	Partner, Exchange, Unite, Brainstorm	Consult, Probe, Confer, Collaborate
Low Commonality	Discount, Disregard, Ignore, Avoid	Critique, Compete, Resist, Disdain

We should not turn a blind eye to or to gloss over differences, since new points of view are enlightening. But we should seek mutual goals and advance understanding whenever possible. And to accomplish that, we must first learn and respect what the other party seeks. While it is tempting, we cannot merely assert our own viewpoint or goals. When we want collaboration and innovation, it is also wise to deemphasize status or title distinctions. Demonstrating respect stimulates a reciprocal search for mutually satisfactory solutions.

It is through listening that we build respect for another and find common ground for constructive engagement.

Walk in Another's Footsteps

Whether we walk in others' shoes, moccasins, or boots, we choose to travel their path with them to understand what shapes their thinking. Before we judge others or exhort them to change, we must grasp the lens they currently use to see their reality. Atticus Finch in *To Kill A Mockingbird* counseled his daughter by saying, "You never really understand a person until you consider things from his point of view, until you climb inside of his skin and walk around in it."

Walking in another's shoes not only helps us gain insights and wisely apply them to resolve conflict, it helps us learn how to influence others to gain their active involvement. Needless to say, influence and involvement forestalls conflict. Dale Carnegie provided an interesting example when he told the following story in his book *How to Win Friends & Influence People.*

"Personally I am very fond of strawberries and cream, but I have found that for some strange reason, fish prefer worms. So when I went fishing, I didn't think about what I wanted. I thought about what they wanted. I didn't bait the hook with strawberries and cream. Rather, I dangled a worm or grasshopper in front of the fish and said: 'Wouldn't you like to have that?' Why not use the same common sense when fishing for people?"

This is the classic win-win approach. When we give others what they cherish, reciprocity provides us with our desired outcomes.

A MINDSET APPROACH TO GAINING INFLUENCE

As we have seen, we can reduce unnecessary and unproductive conflicts by: 1) gaining insights into another's current mindsets, and 2) finding common ground to reduce the potential for serious clashes.

However, we can manage unproductive conflict by using our *influence*, which we can also call power, leverage, sway, pull, or weight. Influence is not a one-size-fits-all process since there are many sources, and what works in one situation may be inappropriate in another.

What we term "authority-based influence" translates into position power and results in compliance. Authority in the form of expertise is much more likely to gain active support and commitment. Likewise, personality-based influence should not be misinterpreted as laying on the charm or back slapping since the impact is short lived. If that is attempted, it will quickly be followed by buyer's remorse. To quote Peter Senge: "Nothing living will obey." There is a difference between temporary agreement and full commitment. Relationship or rapport influence is a different story. It has lasting impact. The only downside to relationship power is that it requires time to build.

Focus on Bottom-Line Influence

Neither position authority or relationship influence is sufficient in today's organizations where we want both fast and lasting alignment. We need to increase our influencing portfolio to what is called "Bottom-Line Influence." This does not require personal history, formal authority, charm, or a long history of personal bonds. Instead, Bottom-Line Influence delivers what the other party wants in ways that also gives us what we seek. It is mindset based.

The advantage of understanding and including the other party's reality is it engenders commitment that lasts. Mutual understanding focuses energy, stirs creative thinking, builds resilience, and ensures effective follow-through.

In addition, our use of Bottom-Line Influence sustains effort and maintains resiliency. Everyone becomes more efficient, creative, and focused on sharing information, exploring options, and finding new choices rather than dealing with how to handle objections or developing PowerPoint presentations. Bottom-Line Influence examines the audience's concerns, assumptions, and mindsets. After all, it is easier to gain interest at the start rather than having to revive it later. First impressions carry weight.

Follow the Platinum Rule

While the Golden Rule encourages us to give unto others based on what we want to receive, another principle underlies Bottom-Line Influence: the Platinum Rule. It advocates giving others what they want, and it requires that we identify the "what's-in-it-for-them" factor. After all, we can use moving phrases and inspirational speeches to spark interest, but that has a temporary effect. Instead, we can listen and help them get what they seek, which will trigger a reciprocal interest in giving us what we seek. We reciprocate when others offer to assist us and search for ways to merge our interests. We can accomplish a great deal when both parties are bent on helping each other.

The aim of Bottom-Line Influence is not to win over hearts or win accolades for intellectual prowess. Instead, it examines desired outcomes, explores new options, and exposes outdated thinking. At the core of results-focused influence is an apparent oxymoron: steadfast flexibility. It gives us the opportunity to flexibly solve the other person's issues to meet our own steadfast goals.

Engage in Win-Win Thinking

Either/or, win-lose or zero-sum thinking dominates interactions. We assume that one party's gains come at our expense. However, there is another option: the kind of win-win outcome that provides mutual goal achievement.

The story about two youngsters arguing over an orange illustrates the point. A compromise using zero-sum thinking is to divide the orange evenly between them. If there is concern over whether it could be fairly split, you assign the task of dividing to one child knowing that the other child will select his half first. This "solution" accepts the premise that each child will be disappointed to some degree in return for some satisfaction.

How might a Bottom-Line Influence approach change the outcome? It would start by seeking a clearer understanding of the desired outcomes. For example, let's say one youngster wanted orange juice and would discard the pulp and rind, while the other wanted the rind for his mother to decorate a cake.

Now a new alternative surfaces, and it fully satisfies both parties. In fact, it doubles the usefulness of the orange. Instead of using two oranges to meet the needs, one orange is sufficient. Exploring the goals and context often reveals such win-win options.

To use a geometric analogy, consider one person at one end of a continuum labeled as point A and the other at the other end labeled point B.

A   **B**

Starting from opposite end points, we commonly assume a compromise at or near the continuum's midpoint.

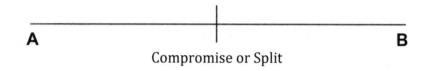

A   **B**

Compromise or Split

Since each party gains some territory, this at first appears reasonable and a win-win solution. In reality, it is a lose-lose resolution. While both parties are initially happy the dispute has been settled, both wonder if they might have obtained more. They are left to consider if there was another argument they could have advanced or if they should have held out longer. Was there something else they could have included that would have made a difference? Will others see this settlement as weakness or failure? Over time we grow more dissatisfied with the compromise and enter the realm of "buyer's remorse."

Bottom-Line Influence offers a true win-win. It expands the scope to expose new options. Stepping back and looking at an issue from a different perspective yields new choices that are more than just a blending or mixing of the original positions. Finding new alternatives from even polar opposite positions was encapsulated by Georg Hegel, who posited that an original thesis produces an opposite, or antithesis, which produces a novel synthesis. Unanticipated insights appear when there is a shift in time, an expansion or limitation of territory, a new scope of work, a change in specifications, additional or reduced services, technological breakthroughs, additional participants, or new parameters.

To illustrate this principle, let's revisit the A and B position at extreme points along a line. There is an option of taking the issues to a new plane or, in this instance, a new point. The C apex is derived from openly exploring mindsets and fully satisfies A and B goals.

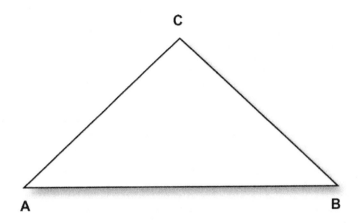

An international example reflects this principle in action. Israel and Egypt held opposing views and goals. However, in the 1978 Camp David negotiations, there was an agreement which, at the outset, appeared unlikely. The starting point for both Israel and Egypt was complete control of the Sinai Peninsula. While the land mass was defined, there were other areas for exploration. For example, Israel's Menachem Begin wanted the land to secure Israel from attacks, while Egypt's Anwar Sadat wanted sovereignty for the land to be returned to Egypt after the Six Day War or the Third Arab-Israeli War. (When the name of the event cannot be agreed upon, disagreement is evident.)

In the end, a mutually satisfying agreement was struck. Rather than giving half the land to each party, security was assured by demilitarizing the area. This met Israel's prime concern, and the sovereignty or governance of the Sinai was returned to Egypt.

Sometimes mindset-based influence can be used to address even deeply felt conflicts. Consider the two different views on abortion that have proved so divisive. The "right to life" movement sought to stop abortions, while others who supported "freedom of choice" wanted to offer women the option of a safe abortion. Both groups employed media, fund raising, legal strategies, and legislative lobbying to win support.

How likely would it be that these two groups could find common ground? Surprisingly, they could. The Search for Common Ground brought members from the pro-life and pro-choice groups together to mutually agree to help prevent teenage pregnancies, promote adoption, support expectant mothers, and reduce infant mortality rates. By reframing the issue, both groups agreed to partner to tackle tough issues.

Leverage the Mindset Framework

Business leaders regularly struggle with situations that seem to be binary choices—only two options are possible. But few situations only have two options. There are nearly always creative solutions waiting to be discovered. For example, a small-business owner leased 20,000 square feet of space for twenty years. Five years into his lease, he shifted his business model. The new business model would require fewer staff and less space. He approached his landlord about cutting his space to 10,000 square feet. Understandably, the landlord was unwilling to modify the lease, since it would mean a loss of income. A fifty percent reduction in his $400,000 per year lease was not in his best interest. A mutually frustrating standoff was averted when both sides agreed to investigate mutual satisfaction.

The two sides recast the debate from modifying an existing lease to creating a new lease at the higher current rate per square foot. The going rate of $22 per square foot was $2 higher than the rate negotiated five years ago. The business owner offered to pay the increased fee for 10,000 square feet, giving the landlord $220,000 along with the option of finding a tenant for the other half of the space, which would produce an income of $440,000, or a net ten percent increase. The business owner, although paying more per square foot, reduced his rent from $400,000 to $220,000 for a forty-five percent savings.

Stark differences can also afflict organizations. An international firm confronted a dilemma: a business cycle retrenchment necessitated a reduction in the highly trained staff. The need to cut staff conflicted with a long-standing commitment to job security. Given either-or thinking, discussions centered on what positions to cut, when to take reductions, how to announce them, and what severance package to offer. As discussions continued, rumors about the impending decision spread. Some became angry, but others elected to search for new alternatives.

Four options were presented to management including: (1) offer six- to twelve-month unpaid sabbaticals for those who wanted to attend school or take an extended vacation, (2) provide part-time jobs or reduced work schedules to those who had family responsibilities, (3) offer early retirements to those nearing retirement, and (4) present those who might want to start their own business the opportunity to pursue a startup with the option of either coming back to the firm or doing business with the firm. All of the choices were open to volunteers, and enough people elected to accept the offers that a layoff was averted, morale increased, and the organization obtained flexibility for a rapid gear up when the economy recovered.

Remember that Turf Battles Start in the Mind

Organizational turf battles reflect a zero-sum mentality. Different units fight for "their" budget, based on pride and competitive posture. Unit leaders jockey for promotions, not recognizing that their Lone Ranger act negatively impacts their professional standing. There are firms that encourage internal competition, but that means that when a person does not win the promotion, he or she feels compelled to leave the firm.

Professional or functional turf battles are also common. Consider the case of a precision machinery company that manufactured printing press equipment and developed a breakthrough digital-to-plate technology. Despite great enthusiasm in the engineering department, the design was not well received in sales and marketing. From an Inventing Mindset viewpoint, the benefits of the new press were compelling, including advantages such as short "make-ready" time, finer screening capability, and reduced maintenance cost.

From the point of view of sales staff operating from the Catalyzing Mindset, however, the new press threatened relationships with key customers. Two years earlier, the sales force had encouraged customers to buy new equipment with the promise that that equipment would be state-of-the-art for decades. So they were reluctant to present their customers with new technology after so recently promising that the last upgrade would last for years. They were also worried that they would alienate their small- to mid-size customer base by presenting an expensive new press. Therefore, they strenuously objected to releasing the new equipment.

Harsh rhetoric and false attributions flew back and forth until having exhausted every polar position, they decided to expand their thinking. The solution was found when they adopted the Challenging Mindset and found a new business model—buying and selling used presses. This allowed customers who made recent purchases to upgrade to the new technology and recoup some of the cost by selling their existing equipment. This approach not only served customers, but also enlarged sales opportunities and encouraged further innovation. All sides quickly got on board.

This is a good example of "reframing" problems to accommodate multiple mindsets. Leaders who can reframe initiatives influence thinking and align energies. Reframing encompasses many forms: expanding or contracting the scope, asking parties to iteratively apply new mindsets, encouraging blue sky thinking, listening to customers, forging new business partnerships, or focusing on innovation. Such leaders know how to enlarge scope and capture synergistic opportunities that advance the interests of all parties.

Just a word of caution on the true value of your brilliant idea: it is zero without effective implementation. In fact, it is better to accept a more mediocre plan that would be actively supported and executed. After all, the brightness of the idea does not count if it never materializes. While a few will admire those who can craft a dazzling prospect, success is not measured by the wattage of the idea but by gleaming results.

KEY STEPS IN USING BOTTOM-LINE INFLUENCE

By exercising the mindset influence approach, we uncover new options, connections, and synergies. This type of influence requires a flexible and inquisitive process. It requires us to withhold our support for a specific idea until all considerations have been identified. We need time to unearth new solutions, fresh data, and vital interfaces.

This method of gaining influence invests time upfront to analyze interests rather than "selling" a predetermined solution. Yet, it is a wise choice, since finding a better solution and gaining commitment at the start expedites execution and reduces the need for do-overs later.

Those who say there is not time to get it right at the start usually find the time later when they have to fix problems. Exploring up front defines what is possible, what implications there are for existing systems, what new interfaces are needed, what schedule is required, what new roles and responsibilities are needed, what risks may surface, and what standards and measures are used to gauge success.

The investment of time to deeply dig into an issue yields the following:

- The identification of new solutions (achieved by expanding the scope of inquiries rather than by sticking to one position)
- Improving decision quality through vigorous inquiry across mindsets
- Enhancing cooperation and creativity
- Producing high levels of commitment
- Faster implementation

Because this process negates the need for grandiose promises, camouflaged agendas, unanticipated bottlenecks, or late objections, implementation is more likely to be on time and on budget. This smooth rollout springs from knowing the contingencies and ramifications before launch and reduces the likelihood of derailment.

However, this approach requires courage. We must be confident in our ability to handle difficult questions, admit that there are unknowns, and start a conversation that will likely challenge cherished best practices as well as assumptions held by regions, units, customers, or project managers.

Steps in Using Bottom-Line Influence

1. Recognize which mindsets currently drive others.
2. Determine your desired outcomes and mindset.
3. Expand the choices by considering each mindset.
4. Collect data from all mindsets.
5. Select the best solution for all parties.
6. Plan, communicate, and implement the solution.
7. Monitor and evaluate the results and then celebrate success.

The first two steps address understanding current mindsets and desired outcomes. The best way to determine these is to get first-hand information from direct inquiry. If that is not feasible, use the Profile Predictor. After determining what drives others, we can translate current thinking into desired outcomes. Next, determine what is driving us and then distinguish our "must have" needs from the "nice to have" desires. What might we be willing to give up in order to obtain something more critical?

The third step also tends to challenge conventional methods—finding creative alternatives and avoiding any tendency to merely split two entrenched points of view. Whether the solution unfolds through careful analysis or suddenly materializes, new possibilities form when boundaries and constraints are removed. Some questions that promote creative exploration include:

- What could happen if time frames or resources changed?
- What has been overlooked?
- Can the scope be increased or decreased?
- What does success look like? What are the tangible outcomes?
- What can we all agree to at this time?
- What are the one or two nonnegotiable aspects?
- What areas of our current practices can be leveraged in this situation?
- What metaphors might be applied?
- What can we learn from our or others' best practices?
- Who can be included or consulted?
- What is our real timeframe for making this decision?
- How can territory/scope/size be expanded or limited?
- Can the specifications or requirements shift?
- Are stages or phases appropriate?

After expanding potential alternatives, it is time to collect information from as many perspectives as possible. Data collection must follow creative exploration so that the "traditional" response will not become the *defacto* response. We must test unconventional ideas for feasibility. Too often, alternatives and ideas are limited to the tried-and-true, which is usually more

[194]

money or more people. Even when conflicting information surfaces, we still benefit since we can separate fact from opinion and clarify what factors take precedence.

There are many techniques for selecting the best solution. Despite the enthusiasm or excitement engendered by an innovative solution, the process for gaining acceptance is arduous. Sometimes the "not invented by me" syndrome interferes but, more frequently, it is the newness or untested nature that raises concerns. Therefore, we must define the decision-making process and gain acceptance for it prior to making a decision. Decision processes do differ. Some identify the evaluation criteria and then use a multi-rater process, while others use a forced-choice process. Actually, it doesn't matter which process is used as long as everyone agrees to adopt it beforehand.

The final two steps are the most familiar since they involve planning, communicating, implementing, monitoring, and recognizing progress. One note of caution about the word "resistance": avoid the label. When we use labels, we discount others. Frequently, the person who is asking the hard questions is merely trying to understand the plan. Asking for more information is not resistance, it is interest.

Stressing the Benefits

We tend to spotlight and stress the broad advantages of any new plan, but that is not sufficient. We must also get down into the weeds with issues such as: what is the time line, who will be responsible for the project, what resources will be assigned, and when and where will it roll out? These details enable others to judge how beneficial the plan is to their unit, their customers, or their career. We must articulate what benefits will be obtained rather than assume that a broad brush and generalities work. Keep in mind that understanding what's-in-it-for-me is not a matter of guesswork or mind reading. It can be detected and predicted.

While desired outcomes can be discerned by mindset, another analysis can be conducted by organizational position. There are reaction patterns to change. Executives typically prefer centralized solutions, which enable them to be in touch with as much information as possible. Middle managers favor decentralization so they can respond quickly to change. Front-line employees seek clear standards and measures to guide their actions while also enhancing their autonomy. In essence, each group seeks an outcome that puts responsibility on their shoulders.

To effectively communicate the benefits, we need to decipher the goals that each type of mindset tends to value. This does not require mind-reading abilities or Sherlock Holmes' skills of deduction. Indicators of mindsets can be gleaned from:

1. Listening for patterns in questions and concerns. These will reflect the outcomes that appeal to the speaker or group.
2. Eliciting input from implementers about potential pitfalls that might derail the plan or limit its success.
3. Reviewing the desired outcomes sought by each mindset using the Recommended Strategies Table (see Table Five).

When we are in a position that requires us to address a large or diverse group, we must include aspects of all six mindsets.

Bottom Line Influencing in Action

A few years ago a large firm elected to upgrade its technology. The matter was considered so critical that the decision was made without extensive debate, fanfare, notice, or preparation. In fact, it was introduced over a weekend when all equipment could be replaced efficiently. On Monday morning, an all-employee meeting was held to introduce the new technology with the stated goal that the new equipment would improve productivity. Features such as faster access to data, more ergonomic keyboards, and automatic error messages were touted. The new equipment required minor schedule changes, but major changes in factors such as office layout or staff levels were not required. Since nothing *really* changed, it was assumed that the change would be readily accepted as positive. That hope was quickly dashed when the audience was asked if there were any questions. Slowly the questions started and the tension level increased. Concerns focused on:

- What schedule changes will there be? Will I have the same work and lunch hours?
- Will new teams be formed?
- Will I be reporting to a new supervisor?
- Will there be split shifts?
- Who will decide the new schedules? Will people be given a choice?

It was clear. Technology was not the major stumbling block to acceptance. Rather, the questions reflected the Protecting Mindset as employees tried to figure out if it would disrupt their team dynamics, reporting relationships and personal networks.

Unfortunately, top management had not gotten into these "details" and, therefore, could not immediately respond to the concerns. Their leaders had focused so completely on the big picture that they felt rollout details could be addressed later, which is a common mistake. While they wisely promised to get answers quickly, the leaders looked ill prepared which just stoked the flame of concern. It was a clear setback.

If top leaders had applied a mindset framework, their planning and communication would have prepared them for those questions. Unfortunately, the leaders' focus on efficiency, technology, and logistics had consumed their time and energy, causing them to appear flat-footed when it counted. Eventually things smoothed out, but it took a few months and more conversation.

One way to detect mindsets and prepare to address corresponding concerns is to use the Recommended Strategies table (see Table Five). It identifies the likely goal that is being sought and also how we might focus on that mindset in our communication. The focus column also serves as a checklist to ensure that all mindsets have been included during early deliberation as well as in the preparation of the communication strategy. After all, when we lead the conversation by speaking about other people's concerns, we usually make them more comfortable and willing to reciprocate.

In addition, the table suggests specific communication approaches or methodologies. When communicating with large audiences, we should consider all mindsets in our communication strategy. The table highlights the need for multiple messages and formats that can be incorporated into a communication plan.

All too often, change-related communication strategies boil down to mass emails, CEO exhortations about an impending crisis, huge gatherings, pleas for loyalty, winning over informal influencers, videoconferences, or PowerPoint presentations to each unit. Impressive as this list is, it is not sufficient without feedback opportunities, clear metrics, and the potential to modify a major initiative. Unfortunately, most organizations only deploy multiple approaches after a single, focused "easy sell" plan fails.

To fully grasp the challenge of gaining support from a large group, review the last two columns on the chart: Communications Approach and Expectation. It is evident that there are conflicting expectations, reflecting a need for an inclusive communication plan. This often runs contrary to planners' wish to get things moving quickly. The desire for quick implementation is understandable since the planners have lived with the decision for a while and are anxious to get the ball rolling. Planning cannot stop at merely burrowing into the details. In actuality, both a deep and broad examination are necessary to craft an effective communication plan.

When dealing with individuals or smaller groups, we can deliver a tailored presentation. Some of us use a pre-meeting process to gauge the reception and test how to sway an individual or small groups. The pre-meeting meeting enables us to make small adjustments, gain ownership by presenting the plan as a work in progress rather than a *fait accompli* and gain support from key influencers. Early briefings also allow time for people to connect the dots, digest content, verify the details, and collect endorsements. Integrated or larger proposals require complete analysis, fuller understanding, detailed pre-planning, creative thinking and flexibility. In short, a full exploration of mindsets improves planning and acceptance from large or diverse groups.

Table Five: Recommended Strategies

	RECOMMENDED STRATEGIES			
Mindset	**Goal**	**Focus**	**Communication Approach**	**Expectation**
Inventing	Develop new products or services; extend product lines	Emerging discoveries and technologies, syntheses, nontraditional alternatives	Written documentation and personal ex-changes	Extensive exploratory discussions and continued involvement
Catalyzing	Grow by gaining new customers and retaining existing customers; respond quickly to the market	Present time, immediate action, new customer opportunities, beating the competition	Personal assurance that success will be attained, flexibility and responsiveness to new requirements or expectations	Rapid decision making, encouragement and varying levels of involvement
Developing	Create structures and systems to attain excellence; use internal talent & clear policy to guide decisions	Clear relationships and roles, broad perspective, accountabilities	Clear logic, clear roles and responsibilities, communication flow	Delegation and autonomy, creation of systems to support initiative

Table Five: Recommended Strategies (cont.)

		RECOMMENDED STRATEGIES		
Mindset	Goal	Focus	Communication Approach	Expectation
Performing	Optimize results and efficiencies; create standardized operating practices	Improved quality control, cost-benefit analysis, waste reduction, process improvement	Written analysis of data or charts displaying performance levels, comparison data across industry or time; effective problem solving	Delegated implementation, management by exception
Protecting	Maintain culture and tradition; develop people and morale; maintain organizational health	Community stewardship, identifying risk, explore ramifications, talent management, organizational reputation	Use informal communication, show compatibility of initiative with culture, acceptance of key individuals/groups, valuing people as key resource, grooming talent	Consultative deliberations, cautious decision making
Challenging	Develop long-term vision and strategy; seize new business opportunities and/or models	Emerging trends and technologies, validating operational assumptions, examining scenarios, learning from experience	Big picture thinking, need for change, multiple data sources	Acceptance of contradictory input, creative proposals, design involvement, delegated implementation

SUMMARY AND NEXT APPLICATION

Using this mindset-based approach to influence, we are better positioned to win support for new initiatives, turning a promising idea or proposal into a much more likely reality.

Now that we know how to use mindsets to influence others, the next step is to use it to increase effectiveness. Just as mindsets channel individual thinking and action, teams develop mindsets, too. Knowing how to leverage a team's mindset ensures that its strengths are captured and potential obstructions are removed. Implementation requires teamwork, and the next chapter explores how to use mindsets to improve team effectiveness.

Harvesting Team Power

Alone we can do so little; together we can do so much.

— *Helen Keller*

Talent wins games, but teamwork and intelligence wins championships.

— *Michael Jordan*

Teamwork is the secret that make common people achieve uncommon result

— *Ifeanyi Enoch Onuoha*

Teamwork is a powerful and attractive concept. Most of us celebrate teams, especially in the field of sports but also in nearly every other field of human endeavor, including the arts, sciences and business.

When teams achieve great and unexpected things, we recognize that the outcomes are far in excess of the individual talents of any of its members. We regale their stories in movies such as *Hoosiers*, *Remember the Titans*, and *Miracle* (the U.S. Olympic Hockey Team victory).

Yet, for all the inspiration we draw from teams, they are far from infallible. Far too often, teams are beset by poor leadership, infighting, and talent attrition. Given the prevalence and importance of teams in today's organizations, we must work to ensure their success. Leveraging the mindset framework is one tool to produce a high-performing team.

THE PROMISE AND PERILS OF TEAMWORK

High-functioning medical teams from the operating room to the ER illustrate how effectively high-performing teams operate. Members communicate directly, execute well-practiced protocols, and go above and beyond the call of duty to ensure successful outcomes. Medical teams react quickly and cohesively to critical situations. The pace may be brutal, but teamwork generally thrives amid the challenges. Results seem almost miraculous. They aren't. Rather, they are the offshoot of training, practice, professional dedication, and a compelling mission.

While media (both news and entertainment) highlight team victories, low-functioning teams persist. Think about the word committee. Like teams, these are collections of individuals who are working together to achieve goals. Yet, committees are notorious for stalemates, delays, low accountability, and ineffective decisions that produce lackluster results. Frequently, they avoid, dilute, or even hinder effective problem solving. Some view committees as dysfunctional teams that are mired in conflict and suffering from poorly defined accountabilities.

We learn how to build high-functioning teams by recognizing not only successful practices but those practices that miss the mark. Let's start by understanding differences in team composition.

TWO KEY CATEGORIES OF TEAMS

Since virtually no can be an expert in all areas of our complex world, teams flourish. Teams bring a variety of skills and viewpoints together to solve problems, handle uncertainty, and contain risk. Members from various organizational units, functions, or stakeholder groups contribute by bringing together both orthodox and some less mainstream viewpoints.

These broad-based teams are so popular that many movies and television shows employ plots where a diverse team of colorful individuals solve crimes, create solutions to problems, or deliver justice. Consider the famous Star Trek series, where an action-oriented and task-driven leader teams up with a data-driven science officer and a caring medical professional. Team members balance out each other so that, as a unit, they can effectively handle unexpected and unknown situations.

Another key type of team is made up of people with similar specialized expertise. For example, a team of electrical engineers may be needed to work out a complex microprocessor design. Typically, the common backgrounds among team members allow them to quickly build respect and a common understanding. Specialized teams, therefore, often deliver fast and decisive action aimed at problem resolution, risk assessments, and operational issues.

These two categories of teams remind us of the classic proverb by Greek poet Archilochus: "The fox knows many things, but the hedgehog knows one big thing." That is, the fox—like the broad-based team—knows many things, while the hedgehog—like the specialized team—knows one big thing very well. When we form teams, we need to consciously select the type that meets our needs.

"Hedgehog teams" tend to have a narrow focus and include: (1) the continuous work team that has an ongoing responsibility within the organization, (2) the temporary task team—also called tiger, red, or "A" team—which is formed to quickly solve a problem and then disband, and (3) the many self-managed teams that perform a continuing task for the organization without close supervision. All of these teams have clear expectations about what outcomes they need to achieve.

"Fox teams" address broad areas by tapping multiple areas of functional knowledge. They tend to include: (1) decision-making teams that are required to tackle unprecedented challenges, (2) executive teams formed by leaders of different functions driven by a common organization-wide goal, and (3) communication teams which are expected to funnel information to others, without any true decision-making capability.

THE POWER OF TEAM MINDSETS

We have long sought the secrets to high-performing teams. At first, our attention was drawn to team dynamics with an examination of team roles and communication. Team-building activities centered on preparing the members to work effectively together by building trust and clarifying expectations.

In some cases, organizations have sent team members to team-building retreats where they engaged in outdoor challenges, experiential exercises, and building personal connections. But the benefits often prove temporary as team members return to their normal work setting and routine.

A more sustainable impact can be produced by using the mindset framework we've discussed throughout this book.

Using the Mindset Framework to Achieve Team Balance

Teams sometimes fail because of narrow or fixed viewpoints. For example, project teams made up of specialized information technology (IT) experts may find that they fail to consider critical elements in the eyes of their non-tech customers. One solution is to include client representatives at the start of an IT project to bolster alignment and build buy-in for change in the client's organization.

Just a Minor IT Modification Case

To illustrate the need for broader team membership, consider the situation where one IT team planned for a "minor" database change. The team planned to introduce Microsoft SharePoint software to its organization. It was expected this should take no more than six months. It was considered a minor transition that they expected to easily introduce to the entire organization all at once. They were wrong.

Users did not immediately accept the cloud-based document-storage-and-collaboration system. This reaction was due, in part, to fear that documents would be lost or that the documents would not be secure from inappropriate access. In addition, the requirement to learn and use a uniform protocol was seen as a hassle.

We can view this from a mindset framework. On one hand, the IT team valued the following features: improved site management, reduced need for storage capacity, greater opportunities for networking, and increased enterprise search capacity. In essence, they used a Performing Mindset to plot a seamless transition to a new protocol.

Instead, users responded with concerns about their ability to control their work product and the required changes in their work practices. In fact, many complained that it was a "big brother" initiative. They wanted to keep doing things in the same way and to remain in control. They were seeing the situation from a Protecting Mindset, so the change was not seen as progress. It was threatening. In this case, we see how a "hedgehog" team made up of specialists misunderstood their audience's mindset.

After a difficult first year, IT widened the composition of its team, appointing a change manager to help IT understand other viewpoints. Finally, the transition was accomplished, but time and trust were lost by the team's narrow assumptions and perspectives.

Using the Mindset Framework to Bridge Perspectives

Mindset awareness is just as essential for executive teams as it is for an IT project team. If executives can appreciate another's point of view, a narrow functional orientation can be broadened to build an organizational perspective. Appreciating different mindsets ensures comprehensive analysis, greater cohesion, and more brilliant decisions.

Identifying the Real Source of Tension Case

An executive team had been through extensive team-building efforts and had enjoyed various opportunities for social interaction and bonding. The five members' roles and responsibilities had been clarified and accepted within the team. And an organizational charter provided guidance on expectations.

So, why had the team's performance declined? One reason was that decisions were never final. At every meeting, the "decision" from the past meeting was reopened. The CEO had a theory. She thought the team's problems stemmed from the differences in age and gender. The CEO was a middle-aged woman, and the most contentious member, a VP, was a more senior male.

The CEO hired a facilitator to work out the problems. The primary issue turned out not to be age and gender diversity but mindset differences. The CEO was operating from the Inventing Mindset, whereas the most dissatisfied team member was prioritizing a Performing Mindset. Every time the CEO introduced new ideas, the VP operating from the Performing Mindset would ask practical questions, such as how resources would be reallocated, when the initiative would start, and what results were expected in the first six months. The stress in shifting between exploring new ideas and attending to implementation issues made both parties uncomfortable. The CEO felt that the questions were designed to demonstrate that she had not carefully analyzed critical aspects, while the VP felt that sweeping creative ideas introduced unnecessarily vague goals that might be difficult to him to fulfill. When they came to understand that they were operating from different (though equally valuable) mindsets, the issues were depersonalized. Respect for the other party's contributions grew as did the ability to set and maintain a course of action. The process of constantly revisiting issues ended. Recognizing the VP's ability to translate broad plans into actual progress, the CEO's reliance on the VP's input increased along with team performance.

Understanding the value of each mindset dramatically improved team interactions. Demographic labels and stereotypes evaporated. The mindset approach benefited the VP's career. He was promoted four months later to SVP.

Mindsets and Team Building

Team clashes occur frequently as they face uncertainty, challenges, and complexity. Consider an example of a cross-functional team in an established international service firm that was chartered to improve results by ten percent in two years. Clearly, this could only happen through creative thinking and new initiatives. It was a steep challenge for a firm proudly and firmly rooted in its old ways. Even modifying its corporate font had been viewed as a serious change.

So, at the outset, the Project Leader understood the challenge and decided a team-building session was necessary, using the mindset-based *Leadership Spectrum Profile®*.

Team members found that they were prioritizing different mindsets. The Project Leader and two other members approached the task from an Inventing Mindset. The other four members had adopted a Performing Mindset for this task. As you'll recall from the last chapter, these two mindsets are opposite each other on the Spectrum Wheel.

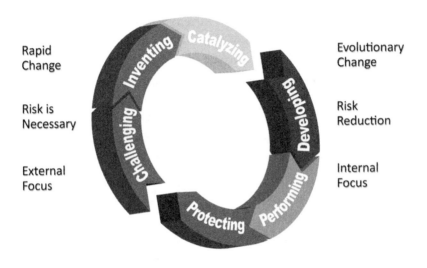

Rapid
Change

Risk is
Necessary

External
Focus

Evolutionary
Change

Risk
Reduction

Internal
Focus

Figure Five: Hemisphere Orientations

There are good reasons why these mindsets are difficult to mesh. Inventing Mindsets focus primarily on external factors while Performing Mindsets are internally focused. This means that those with Inventing Mindsets want to discover new ideas while those with Performing Mindsets favor reliance on tested, proven approaches.

Identifying this dichotomy helped the team. They established practices to ensure that everyone was heard and respected. They used a two-pronged approach to target both breakthrough ideas and incremental change ideas. Even when discussing breakthrough ideas, they considered how those ideas would be viewed from a "right hemisphere" point of view (see Figure Five). Their plan set aside time for data collection and brainstorming and then devoted time to validating, investigating, and evaluating ideas. By providing sufficient time for vetting, risk analysis, and the testing of new ideas, those with the Performing Mindsets felt comfortable. As a result, confidence and commitment increased. They also checked the four less prominent mindsets at intervals to thwart surprises and prepare their communication plan.

Over time, the team presented their challenging goal to the entire organization and then conducted company-wide brainstorming sessions involving hundreds of people. The effort netted more than 1,800 unduplicated ideas. Armed with a wide array of new—and sometimes unusual—ideas and an immovable deadline for results, the team selected eighty-eight ideas for closer review. Members agreed that their project did not have to rely on one great idea, but could consist of multiple projects that jointly could produce the desired ten percent improvements.

To prevent wallowing in endless discussions, the team developed a motto of "propose, counter-propose, or get out of the way." Whether an idea's impact was large or small, the team examined all options, believing that multiple small efforts could significantly contribute to their success. The result? Several initiatives were launched and the ten percent goal was achieved.

Carefully crafted decisions making practices helped the team sidestep such traps as digressing into divisive debate, ignoring system constraints, endlessly examining data, failing to listen to those who question the feasibility of ideas, making decisions too slowly, and indulging in unproductive conflict.

USING MINDSETS TO AVOID DR. JEKYLL AND MR. HYDE

Figure Five depicts the two mindset hemispheres. As the illustration shows, the mindsets on the right side—Developing, Performing and Protecting—share three common elements. To review the distinctions, the mindsets in the right hemisphere focus internally on the organization, have an interest in reducing risk, and prefer gradual or managed change over rapid, riskier ventures. Whether the internal focus is on infrastructure, process improvement, increased financial success, succession planning, or internal culture, these mindsets generally agree that the best results can be obtained by modifying internal systems.

In contrast, the mindsets in the left hemisphere—Challenging, Inventing and Catalyzing—closely watch external advancements. Attuned to these changes, they conclude that fast action is necessary and that taking on acceptable levels of risk is the path to great results. This hemisphere's goal is to learn about and quickly apply new thinking, new business models, new products, and new market strategies.

In team settings, members operating from different hemispheres are likely to experience tension stemming from these different outlooks. After all, the right hemisphere views rapid change as unrealistic, unworkable, and destructive to a successful track record. Meanwhile, those functioning from the left side consider that view to be wedded to the past, stubborn, and fearful.

Amid such conflicts, mistrust can grow, cliques can form, and stereotypes flourish. As a result, team cohesion suffers, ideas fail to gain traction, morale wavers, and results fall short. Instead of viewing those with a different viewpoint as being from a different planet or as having a dysfunctional view, including all mindsets at the outset creates a firm foundation for progress. Ask the team to identify their mindsets and how each contributes to goal achievement. Team effectiveness benefits from diverse perspectives by debunking false assumptions, revealing new opportunities, and avoiding blunders.

Playing Favorites Case

While it is a challenge to bring a team with a split hemisphere together, it is also tricky to have a team leader who frequently switches his outlook. Teams observe the inconsistency and wonder whether it is due to incompetency, favoritism, or stress. Either way, productivity suffers and rumors proliferate.

There was a situation where a leader managed two divisions. One division dealt with a highly visible and much loved service that the board of directors monitored closely. The other division had been created in the last few years and operated far beneath the board's radar.

The new division had been created to explore new alternatives and was given a separate and growing budget. In contrast, the budget for the established service remained constrained. Team members in the newer unit were being recognized for pursuing "out of the box" ideas. But every new initiative in the established one was squashed.

Since these employees could not understand the "double standard," they referred to their leader as the reincarnated Dr. Jekyll and Mr. Hyde. Eventually, the leader hired a coach to deal with obvious morale and performance issues. As part of the coaching process, the leader completed the *Leadership Spectrum Profile*®. The results showed that the leader had a split profile, not a split personality, in which he simultaneously prioritized the Inventing Mindset for the newer unit and the Protecting Mindset for the established one.

During the debrief, the leader recognized that his mindset and actions reflected the board's tight scrutiny over his established team. It was seen as critical to delivering on the organization's mission and the board did not want anything to change, especially since it might reflect negatively on the entire operation. Therefore, he had supported only tried-and-true practices to avoid any disruption or disturbance. Likewise, the board's plan for the new team stressed innovation. Therefore, his leadership and level of autonomy for the new team stood in stark contrast to the other more constrained team.

At a joint team meeting, he shared the mindset framework and how the different missions drove his action. This punctured assumptions that he was playing favorites or suffered from severe mood swings. And, it provided all members with a better understanding of the board's role and viewpoint along with opening a healthy discussion on ways to move forward.

USING MINDSETS TO UNDERSTAND TEAM COMPOSITES

In order to build high-performing teams, we need to share how mindsets impact team operations. A composite team mindset obtained from collecting each team member's mindset (with or without attribution to specific individuals) opens discussion. It also serves to examine a team's strengths and potential liabilities.

In a majority of cases, task team members share mindsets from the same basic hemispheres, though in different combinations. Therefore, there are four likely Team Composites:

- Combination of Inventing and Catalyzing Mindsets (in left hemisphere)
- Combination of Developing and Performing Mindsets (in right hemisphere)
- Combination of Performing and Protecting Mindsets (in right hemisphere)
- Combination of Challenging and Inventing Mindsets (in left hemisphere)

Team mindset composites identify areas that may be emphasized and depict areas that might be overlooked or under-appreciated. Aware of these current proclivities, the team can intentionally examine missing mindsets before finalizing a decision. By removing their mindset blinders, a comprehensive, context-driven analysis and effective decision are assured.

Using the Right Teams for the Right Purposes

The good news is that any potential inattention to a mindset can easily be addressed. The team charged with identifying ways to achieve a ten percent improvement mentioned above benefited from revisiting the four mindsets that were not currently dominant. They used a mindset checklist (presented below) to confirm their analysis and plans.

The need for comprehensive review does *not* mean that we have to find one team member with each mindset. Instead of being a Chinese menu where you have to pick from each category, mindsets are not entrees or personalities. Therefore, all that *is* required is the consideration of data from all perspectives to ensure comprehensive analysis and to avoid pitfalls.

The Inventing/Catalyzing Composite

To gain familiarity with how team composites function, let's start with a team where members' priorities converge primarily on Inventing and Catalyzing mindsets. The strength of teams in Figure Six in this instance would include:

- Identifying new products/services to meet the evolving market needs
- Exploring service, product, or market options and opportunities
- Discovering new synergies within current offerings

Figure Six: The Inventing/Catalyzing Composite

This composite fits teams responsible for product innovation, product design, business development, market research, and product launches. Meanwhile, the potential liabilities of this team might include:

- Weak follow-through on ideas or proposals
- Poorly analyzed or resourced implementation plans
- Missed deadlines or overly optimistic time lines

The Challenging/Inventing Composite

In Figure Seven, the team concentrates on Challenging and Inventing Mindsets and its strengths would include:

- Identifying new business models, niches, or product opportunities
- Supporting rapid action and risk taking for future gain
- Recognizing potential alliances, partnerships, or cross-functional opportunities to meet current trends

Figure Seven: The Challenging/Inventing Composite

This team alignment matches teams tasked with identifying emerging opportunities, examining potential partnerships, encouraging strategic thinking, discovering new products, updating assumptions, finding new distribution channels, and defining new business models. Potential deficiencies for this team might include:

- Ignoring system constraints and traditions
- Being excessively optimistic about the probability for success
- Misjudging costs, resource availability, timeline, or level of commitment

[215]

The Developing/Performing Composite

When the team's mindsets cluster in the Developing and Performing Mindsets, the team's strengths illustrated in Figure Eight include:
- A strong goal and outcome orientation
- Attention to systems, networks, processes, costs, workflow, and accountabilities
- An ability to monitor and measure progress

Figure Eight: The Developing/Performing Composite

This team composite suits teams tasked with process or quality improvement, cost benefit analysis, system and process re-engineering, executing projects, and setting metrics and standards. Potential shortcomings might include:

- An overreliance on tested practices and established processes
- Discounting of cultural norms
- Inattention to external demands
- Sluggish decision making

The Performing/Protecting Composite

When a team's driving mindsets center on the Performing and Protecting Mindsets as shown in Figure Nine, the team's strengths deal with:

- Getting things done
- Understanding procedures, practices, and required competencies

- Building skills and a high performing culture

Figure Nine: The Performing/Protecting Composite

This team composite fits teams charged with improving work practices, maximizing safety, focusing on quality, creating effective teams, retaining talent, building bench strength, and fostering pride and unity. Potential shortcomings might include:

- Overestimating the effectiveness of existing formal systems and policies
- Resisting the need for risk or significant change
- Underestimating market, technological, and business trends

COPING WITH COMPLEX TEAMS

However, not all composite teams are so closely aligned. Some team members operate from different hemispheres. Members might hold opposite priorities. It can become more challenging when the mindsets of sponsors, subject matter experts, or clients are also factored into the equation.

Teams chartered to explore options, prepare analyses, and submit a report can find that their sponsor rejects team recommendations based on a different mindset. In fact, many reports crafted by consultants, internal planners, and marketing professionals collect dust on shelves. Despite fighting for their findings with elaborate slide decks, testimonials from key experts, or lofty promises, it is difficult to sway another's view without including their perspective. Those that are willing to see through the same lens as their sponsor increase their chances of winning support and authorization to take the next step.

Balancing Team Mindset Case

A defense contractor started a new 18-month project to integrate an existing information system with a unified knowledge management and talent management system. The Project Leader identified the need to prioritize Challenging and Inventing mindsets (see left hemisphere in Figure Five). But the leader also recognized that his clients operated from a Developing and Performing Mindset composite (see right hemisphere in Figure Seven). After finding that his team's outlook was primarily oriented toward a Performing Mindset, he realized that disconnects within the staff as well as with the client were likely. He devised systems to prevent this from undermining teamwork.

So what did he do? He assigned his Deputy to monitor the Performing and Protecting Mindsets to prevent the potential for under-weighing those perspectives. As leader, he was concerned that his antennae might not detect signs that relationships were becoming frayed, expectations were becoming unrealistic, or problems were building. He negotiated with the client to confirm that he understood the client's expectations. (Procurement might have missed something.) He then created metrics for each mindset to ensure comprehensive monitoring that would alert him to budding issues. In the end, his attention and pre-planning paid off: the contract was completed on time and the client granted the firm an award fee for quality deliverables.

Teams that take into consideration multiple mindsets are more likely to successfully gain support and authorization to move forward. This does *not* mean that every mindset priority must be represented on a team. But it *does* mean that teams, no matter what mindsets they have prioritized, can ask a series of questions that will help them gain a more balanced perspective.

In essence, the team leader balanced the mindsets given the team's mandate. He continued to stress the Challenging and Inventing Mindsets but he also stayed attune to the other mindsets. His approach is reflected in Figure Ten.

Figure Ten: The Inventing/Challenging Balanced Mindset

Balance is often key to success. Conflicts between people with different mindsets cannot be resolved by pressure or command. If convictions could be easily vanquished, the Inquisition would have been successful in stamping out dissident beliefs. Its failure reveals not only how tenaciously people cling to their beliefs, but also how those in charge can become so transfixed by their goal that balance is lost.

Unfortunately, the traditional response of troubled teams is to rotate participants in and out of the group or exhort everyone to focus on getting the job done. Just adding new people to a team in the belief that the right mix of people will turn things around can be classified as the "Red Cross team-building strategy"—that is, hoping new blood will solve all issues. It doesn't.

Deploying Mindset Checklists

Consider the case of an audit team formed to investigate how to advance organization efficiency and effectiveness. The team composite reflects a strong Performing Mindset composition.

At the start, instead of delving into identify problem spots, they chose to review how other perspectives would approach their tasks. Using key questions from the Challenging Mindset perspective, for example, they ask themselves, "What assumptions are we making?" and "What threats could arise?" Reviewing Catalyzing Mindset, it becomes clear that data from customers must be considered. In addition, the Protecting Mindset highlights the potential to obtain ideas from the workforce that might guide their investigation or separate symptoms from causes.

Although the project team continues using the Performing Mindset, its range of inquiry has expanded along with the probability of success. Many teams charged with enhancing efficiencies focus on the easy-to-find symptoms of inefficiency without searching for root causes or exploring system ramifications.

Just as a pedestrian can start to lose his balance and recover, a team wobble does not have to end in failure. Teams can restore equilibrium by checking each mindset perspective. This process consumes little time and offers substantial rewards. Assumptions are tested, additional metrics are identified, new considerations surface, clear needs are established, and multiple factors are uncovered. Therefore, the team is much more likely to avoid a blunder and discover a brilliant solution.

The following checklist captures the critical concerns from each mindset point of view. Each set advances our understanding of the situation, risk, opportunity, or problem.

From an Inventing Mindset:

- What topics can we brainstorm?
- What "outside the box" thinking can we tap?
- What alternatives are there to our assumed solution?

- If there were no constraints, what could we do?
- What is the ideal product or service?
- How can we take our existing products/services to a new level?
- What can we do differently?
- What new options are open given current technology?

From a Catalyzing Mindset:

- What will help our customer base?
- What is the competition doing?
- What actions are critical now to position us for success?
- What will build our brand or reputation?
- What will grow our share of the market?
- How can we increase our responsiveness and service?
- Are we inspired and ready to act?
- Are we learning from and retaining our key customers?

From a Developing Mindset:

- What are our plans, schedule, and goals?
- What is the best way for us to organize?
- How should communication and information flow?
- What systems need to be improved for better alignment?
- What will improve our monitoring effectiveness?
- What are the key roles?
- What resources are required?
- What types of teams are needed?
- What will ensure smooth execution?

From a Performing Mindset:

- What is the cost/benefit analysis?
- What barriers or bottlenecks are likely?

- Do we have the necessary resources?
- What disruptions might impact performance?
- How can we improve our processes?
- How can we reduce costs or improve cycle time?
- Are our measures timely and effective?
- What will improve our return on investment?
- How can we improve quality?

From a Protecting Mindset:

- What actions can enhance our culture and traditions?
- Do we have the skills/staff we need?
- How do we sustain our commitment to fair and ethical practices?
- Is there a high level of engagement?
- Are rewards/recognition aligned and used as planned?
- Are we developing our talent/bench strength to match our strategy?
- How can we develop leaders?
- Are we fulfilling our values and mission?
- Do we have a change-ready culture?

From a Challenging Mindset:

- Are our current assumptions still valid?
- What threats could arise from emerging trends?
- Are we effectively balancing short- and long-term goals?
- What best practices or after-action insights are we deploying?
- What new business models are possible?
- Are we sufficiently agile?
- How can alliances or partnerships help us?
- What emerging customer expectations and trends need to be addressed?
- Are we using strategic thinking and management across the organization?

By asking these questions, our teams will be less likely to neglect key perspectives and more likely to discover ways to improve effectiveness. Asking questions will also develop a better understanding of and respect for other viewpoints. This is, in the long run, at the heart of effective teamwork.

Of course, all six mindsets are not equal in every situation. For example, if the team's goal is to develop and unveil a new product in order to jumpstart a new venture, team members prioritize the Inventing and Catalyzing Mindsets, giving less attention to the other four mindsets. But those other mindsets cannot be ignored or quickly glossed over, either.

Just as any recipe outlines key ingredients, we recognize that if we leave out one element, we will be unpleasantly surprised. And if we rely excessively on another ingredient, we will also be disappointed. To paraphrase the book *Animal Farm*, some mindsets are more equal than others given current circumstances.

CONCLUDING THOUGHTS

Leadership is a science and an art. The six mindsets we have discussed in this book create a practical decision-making framework, but using them well requires artistic sensibilities and skills. That is, there are nuances that require judgment. When do we shift to a new mindset? When should we step back to validate our analysis? What can we do to communicate how mindsets contribute to decision making? Which mindsets best fit our current situation?

Mindsets provide us with guideposts that help us adjust our thinking and attention, but we must be able to decipher the context, react to emerging needs, and foster agility throughout the organization. We cannot be fixated on one product line, customer base, set of competencies, or business model. We can honor past practices without becoming handcuffed by them. Agility rather than constancy is required. Our environments are constantly changing. Mindsets spur us to regularly update our thinking and assumptions in order to generate brilliant decisions that will help our organizations survive and thrive.

The mindset framework makes it easier for us to succeed in areas such as conflict resolution, communication, alignment, and talent development. By investigating all mindset lenses, we can avoid or reduce the false steps or executive failures that are so prevalent. This success stems from wiser decisions, faster acceptance, smoother implementation, clearer communication, and greater confidence. Operating with the full mindset spectrum also reduces our reliance on chance to get things right. We have the means to make brilliant choices in a fast and complex environment.

Adopting and succeeding with the mindset paradigm takes courage as well as skill. It sometimes feels easier to assume the veneer of polite collaboration rather than make a concerted effort to truly understand other mindsets. Understanding other mindsets may, after all, require us to change our thinking.

But what *feels* like the easiest path can be a blunder. After all, we cannot parrot the same phrases, implement the same plans, or follow the same strategies over and over again, hoping for better results. And, we cannot adopt the ostrich posture of sticking our heads in the sand to avoid uncertainties and complex issues. What has worked in the past is not likely to work in the future. If we do dig into one stance or hide from change, we fail the test of leadership, which is to lead our unit or organization to desired results with high levels of commitment in a complex world. If we are able to provide such leadership, then perhaps we too will produce outcomes that can be described as brilliant.

About the Author

Dr. Mary Lippitt, award winning author and consultant, founded Enterprise Management Ltd. in 1985 with the purpose of providing businesses, teams, and organizations with practical and effective solutions to navigate the challenging business climate in the U.S. and internationally.

A hands-on practitioner as well as a researcher, Dr. Lippitt has developed a number of leadership instruments, including the Leadership Spectrum Profile® and its accompanying book, *The Leadership Spectrum: 6 Business Priorities that Get Results*, which won the Bronze award for Best Business Book of 2002. The Leadership Spectrum Profile® won the Human Resource Executive magazines' Top Training Product Award. Other instruments Dr. Lippitt has developed include *Bottom Line Persuasion: Results Focused Influencing*™, *Execution Priorities Inventory*®, and *Leadership Power Levers: Targeting Influence and Motivational Practice*.™

She currently teaches in the M.B.A. program at the University of South Florida, having also taught at George Washington University, Georgetown University, Florida International University, and Saint Thomas University.

Dr. Lippitt is a co-author with Ken Blanchard, Stephen Covey and Brian Tracy of *Discover Your Inner Strengths: Cutting Edge Growth* Strategies *from the Industry's Leading Experts*, published in 2009. Her work on leadership and execution of change has been featured in *Leader to Leader, Executive Excellence,* The *Journal of Business Strategy* and *Industry Week,* as well as in the popular press.

For further information, please contact" mlippitt@enterprisemgt.com
or www.enterprisemgt.com

Bibliography

About Gore. (n.d.). Retrieved August 23, 2014, from http://www.gore.com/en_xx/aboutus/index.html

Anton, W. (2013). *Business success through self-knowledge*. Tampa, FL: HD Interactive.

Ariely, D. (2010). *Predictable irrationality: The hidden forces that shape our decisions*. New York, NY: Harper Perennial.

Bandyk, M. (2010). Business schools' great ethics debate. *Time*. Retrieved from http://money.usnews.com/money/careers/articles/2010/04/16/business-schools-great-ethics-debate

Blumenstein, R. (2001, June 18). How the Fiber Barons Plunged The U.S. Into a Telecom Glut. *Wall Street Journal*. Retrieved from http://online.wsj.com/news/articles/SB992810125428317389

Boyatzis, R. (1982) *The Competent Manager: A Model for Effective Performance*. Hoboken, NJ: Wiley.

Caplin, Jeremy (2006, October). Google's Chief Looks Ahead. *Time*. http://content.time.com/time/business/article/0,8599,1541446,00.html

Collin, C., & Hansen, M. (2011). *Great by choice: Uncertainty, chaos, and luck: Why some thrive despite them all*. New York, NY: Harper Collins Publishers.

Conger, J. (1998). *Winning 'em over: A new model for managing in the age of persuasion*. New York, NY: Simon and Schuster.

Covey, S. (2013). *Seven habits of highly effective people: Powerful lessons in personal change*. 25th edition, New York: Simon & Schuster.

Dewey, J. (1910). *How we think*. Boston: D.C Heath & Co.

Drucker, P. (2006). *The Competent Manager: A Model for Effective Performance*. Revised edition. New York: HarperBusiness.

Duhigg, C. (2012). *The power of habit: Why we do what we do in life and business.* New York, NY: Random House.

Dungy, T. (2008). *Quiet strength: The principles, practices, and priorities of a winning life.* Chicago: Tyndale Momentum.

Finkelstein, S., Whitehead, J., & Campbell, A. (2009). *Think again: Why good leaders make bad decision and how to keep it from happening.* Boston, MA: Harvard Business School Press.

Galbraith, J.R. (2012, March 3) The Future of Organization Design. *Journal of Organization Design.* Retrieved from http://www.jaygalbraith.com/images/whitepapers/GalbraithFutureOrgDesign.pdf

Greenleaf, R. (1998). *The power of servant leadership: Essays.* San Francisco: Berrett-Koehler.

Goleman, D., Boyatzis, R., and McKee, A. (2013) *Primal Leadership, With a New Preface by the Authors: Unleashing the Power of Emotional Intelligence.* 10th edition. Boston: Harvard Business School Press.

Grove, A. (1999) *Only the paranoid survive: How to exploit the crisis points that challenge every company.* New York: Crown Books.

Govindarajan, V., & Trimble, C. (2010). *The other side of innovation: Solving the execution challenge.* Boston Massachusetts: Harvard Business School Publishers.

Heifetz, R. (1994). *Leadership without easy answers.* Cambridge: Belknap Press of Harvard University Press.

Janis, I. (1991). Victims of Group Think. *Political Psychology, 12*(2), 247–278.

Jordan, R., Koljatic, M., & Useem, M. (2011). Leading the rescue of the miners in Chile: Case 66. *The Wharton School of the University of Pennsylvania and Ponitifica Universidad Catholica de Chile.* Retrieved from http://wdp.wharton.upenn.edu/wp-content/uploads/2011/07/Leading-the-Miners-Rescue.pdf

Kahneman, D. (2011). *Thinking, fast and slow.* New York, NY: Farrar, Straus and Giroux.

Kaplan, R., & Kaiser, R. (2006). *The versatile leader: Make the most of your strengths without overdoing it.* San Francisco: Pfeiffer.

Kaplan R. and Norton, D. (1996). *The balanced scorecard: Translating strategy into action.* Boston: Harvard Business Review Press.

Katzenbach, J. (2000). *Peak performance: Aligning the hearts and minds of your employees.* Boston, MA: Harvard Business School Press.

Kegan, R., & Lahey, L. (2000). *How the way we talk can change the way we work: Seven languages for transition.* San Francisco, CA: Jossey-Bass.

Kohn, A. (1999). *Punished by rewards: The* trouble *with gold stars, incentive plans, A's, praise and other bribes.* Boston, MA: Houghton Mifflin Company.

Kouzes, J., & Posner, B. (1995). *The leadership challenge: How to keep getting extraordinary things done in organizations.* San Francisco, CA: Jossey-Bass.

Lippitt, G. (1982). *Organization renewal: A holistic approach to organization development.* Englewood Cliffs, NJ: Prentice-Hall.

Lippitt, G. and Schmidt, W. (1967) *Crises in a Developing Organization.* Boston, MA: Harvard Business Review.

Lippitt, M., Covey, S., Blanchard, K., & Tracey, B. (2009). *Discover your inner strengths.* Sevierville, TN: Insight Publishing.

Marquet, D. (2013). *Turn the ship around!: A true story of turning followers into leaders.* New York: Portfolio Hardcover.

Merrill, D. (2012, August 7). Why multitasking doesn't work. *Forbes.* Retrieved August 8, 2014, from http://www.forbes.com/sites/douglasmerrill/2012/08/17/why-multitasking-doesnt-work/

Nutt, P. (2002). *Why decisions fail: Avoiding the blunder and traps that lead to debacles.* San Francisco, CA: Berrett-Koehler.

Pfeffer, J., & Sutton, R. (2000). *The knowing-doing gap: How smart companies turn knowledge into action.* Boston, MA: Harvard Business School Press.

Pink, D. (2005). *A whole new mind: Moving from the information age to the conceptual age.* New York: Riverhead Books.

Silver, N. (2012). *The signal and the noise: Why so many predictions fail – but some don't.* New York, NY: Penguin Press.

Silverman, R. (2012). Who's the boss? There isn't one, *Wall Street Journal.* Retrieved from http://online.wsj.com/news/articles/SB10001424052702303379204 577474953586383604

Stack, J. (1994). *The great game of business.* New York: Currency Doubleday.

Vaill, P. (1996). *The Competent Manager: A Model for Effective Performance.* San Francisco: Jossey-Bass.

Vaughan, M. (2013). *The thinking effect: Rethinking thinking to create great leaders and the new value worker.* New York, NY: Nicholas Breasley.

Walters, B. (1970). *How to talk with practically anyone about practically anything.* New York: Doubleday.

Index

CPSIA information can be obtained
at www.ICGtesting.com
Printed in the USA
LVOW04s2110200316

479964LV00040B/1499/P